Living in

CHINA

Praying in a temple for good luck

Bronze Bian Zhong, an ancient Chinese palace musical percussion instrument used for ceremonies; it consists of bells of different sizes hung on a large rack and arranged according to pitch. It was uncovered in 1978 in Suixian, Hubei Province, from an early Warring States tomb over 2,500 years old.

Living in

CHINA

Lin Wang
Xiaohua Wei

PRO LINGUA ASSOCIATES

Pro Lingua Associates, Publishers

P. O. Box 1348, Brattleboro, Vermont 05302, USA
Office: 802-257-7779 • Orders: 800-366-4775
Email: info@ProLinguaAssociates.com
WebStore: www.ProLinguaAssociates.com
SAN: 216-0579

Photo credits. Photos by friends of the authors: the front cover photo is by Lin Luo; page ii top Lin Luo, bottom Mr. and Mrs. Rica; p. v Jianguo Xu; p. vi left, p. vi right; p. x top Lin Luo, bottom James Zhou; p. xii top Jianguo Xu, bottom Lijia Wang and Jin Fang; p. 3 Mr. and Mrs. Rica; p. 20 Lin Luo; p. 38 top, bottom & 41 James Zhou, p. 50 Mr. and Mrs. Rica; p. 55 Shaolin Liu; p. 56 top, bottom Lixia Xu; p. 60 top, bottom Mr. and Mrs. Rica; p. 77 Jianguo Xu, p. 80 Lin Luo; p. 83 top, and p. 83 bottom. Photos from the Dreamstime.com Agency: p. 1 left © Zhang Kai, right © Jovan Nikolic, p. 14 © Yali Shi, p. 33 © castaveron, p. 34 © seesea, p. 37 © Jie Xu, p. 39 © Young hian Lim, p. 45 top © Kuan Choong Ng, left © Zina Seletskaya, center © Margot Petrowski, right © Christophe Testi. p. 46 © Paul Hakimata, p. 51 top left © Rotacidni, right © Lint, bottom left © Lihui, right © Franz Pfluegl, p. 67 © Kween Kit Wong. Also p 23 © The Quote Blog.com.

This book was designed and set by Arthur A. Burrows using Adobe Palatino and Cochin display face. It was printed and bound by United Graphics of Mattoon, Illinois.

Printed in the United States of America. First printing 2008. 1500 copies.

Pro Lingua's Living in Series

Living in China • Living in France • Living in Greece
Living in Italy • Living in Japan • Living in Mexico
Living in South Korea • Living in Turkey • Living in the United States

---

The photo on the front cover is of Baima Si, *the White Horse Temple in Luoyang, Henan Province. It was the first Buddhist temple in China, established by Emperor Mingdi in the year 68* A.D. *The lovely garden setting features several ancient buildings and a serenely devotional atmosphere. Mingdi had sent some of his court to India to bring him information about Buddhism, and they returned with two monks and a white horse loaded with sutras and other religious artifacts. To honor the arrival of Buddhism, the emperor built this temple and named it for the white horse. This was an important turning point in Chinese history.*

Bronze Horses and Chariots on page i were made of copper in the Qin Dynasty (221-206 B.C.E.*). They were found in Qin Shi Huang Mausoleum in Xi'an in northwest China's Shaanxi Province in 1980. See pages 55, 56, and 83.*

Acknowledgements

We would like to express our heartfelt thanks to Arnold Stein who has been teaching for many years at our university (Shantou University) and to Elizabeth Gibson, who taught at Shantou University, for their valuable suggestions, ideas, and proofreading of this book. We also extend our sincere appreciation to our professor Dr. Pat Moran at the School for International Training for his great support for this project. We thank our dear daughter Ranran Wang for her understanding and help with our effort to complete this book. We would also like to thank the following friends and relatives for contributing their photos taken in China: Liping He, Shaolin Liu, Lixia Xu, James Zhou, Lin Luo, Rong Zhang, Jianguo Xu, Cong Xie, Mr. and Mrs. Rica, Lijia Wang and Jin Fang. Without their great help and support, this book could never have been completed. And finally, our thanks go to our American students of Chinese who have inspired us to build a bridge of understanding between American and Chinese peoples.

-- *Lin Wang & Xiaohua Wei*

Thanks also to William R. Eubank, Leslie Watson-Eubank, and Zhao Chan for their "Culture Bumps" and comments on the manuscript.

Modern China: The Shanghai skyline by night with the Pearl TV Tower.

Note: In this text we have used the term "North America" to refer primarily to the United States and Canada, although many of the references would also apply to Mexico. In fact, many of the cross-cultural notes would apply to Europe, as well.

Ancient China: The Forbidden City, Beijing.

About the Authors

Lin Wang and Xiaohua Wei have BA's in English from China's Anhui University and MAT's from the School for International Training (SIT), Brattleboro, Vermont. Lin Wang earned his Certificate in Educational Assessment from the University of Cambridge Local Examinations Syndicate (UCLES) in England and his Diploma in Education from Singapore National Institute of Education. Before coming to the U.S., they were associate professors at China's Shantou University. In China they have published bilingual textbooks. In the United States, Lin Wang has taught at the School for International Training, Sandy Spring Friends School in Maryland, and St. Michael's Independent School/ the Pine School in Stuart, Florida, and is currently teaching at the Chapin School in New York. Xiaohua Wei has taught at the Hope Chinese School in Maryland, worked as an international student exchange program manager with Forte International in Washington, D.C., and is currently teaching at Lycée Français de New York. They live in New York City with their daughter Ranran Wang.

Contents

vii

A Note on Pinyin

The Romanized writing of the Chinese language is now done with a system called Pinyin. Simply put, individual sounds in Chinese are represented by Roman letters that are similar to the Chinese sounds. For example the Chinese sound "ah" as in "father" is represented with the Roman letter "a".

However, Chinese is a tonal language, meaning the individual sounds can be spoken with different tones which can be high, low, rising, falling, and combinations such as falling-rising. Four different tone marks are added above the letters to indicate the tone. For example, the first tone , flat or high, is represented with – . Therefore the use of Roman letters alone will not give a completely accurate guide to the pronunciation of words. However, in this book modified Pinyin without tone marks will be used.

The following is a rough guide to the pronunciation of the letters.

The finals (vowels) are basically similar

a as in father	**e** as in up
ai as in high	**ei** as in aid
ao as in how	**i** as in eat
ou as in low	**u** as in food

Most of the initials (consonants) are similar to English, but some are different.

x is like sh in <u>sh</u>e	**q** is like ch in <u>ch</u>eese
z is like ds in be<u>ds</u>	
zh is like j in <u>J</u>une	**c** is like ts as in ca<u>ts</u>

In this book, names in Pinyin will be italicized: *Guangdong*, and the older anglicized spellings will be in parentheses: (Canton).

For more detailed information go to **www.pinyin.org**

Hua Qing Chi, a bathing place for royal families, was discovered more than 2700 years ago in the Western Zhou Dynasty (1046 BC-771 BC). It is located in Xian, Shannxi Province.

Emeishan, Mt. Emei, is one of the four Buddhist sacred mountains of China. It is located in Sichuan Province. Mt. Emei has been designated a World Heritage Site. It's well-known for its breathtaking scenery, mysterious natural wonders, and historical Buddhist sites. It was originally a Taoist retreat, but became a sacred Buddhist mountain by the 3rd century AD.

Introduction

Living in or just visiting China today is an eye-opener, offering you more to see than just a few well-known historic landmarks that have fascinated so many around the world. You will be greeted with the hospitality of 56 ethnic groups throughout the country with their unique cultures and customs, in contrast to only a few places open to foreigners in the 1980's when China had just opened its door to the outside world. These 56 ethnic groups, of which the Han people make up 93.3 percent of the total population, have their own dialects, but they also share a common language that is Putonghua or Mandarin. In section 6 of this book you will find basic Chinese survival language to help you get around.

This book is more than a travel guide; it will help you to understand the past and present of the world's largest population, especially the way Chinese people live, work, and play today. However, it is a changing China that we are presenting to you – China is changing fast, and that must be kept in mind. Nevertheless, we are sure that this book will make it easier for you to work or study, or just to visit China and to communicate with the Chinese people. Above all, we are writing this book to build bridges of understanding and cooperation. China and America are two great nations in the world sharing mutual aspirations of peace and development. Better understanding and cooperation are in the interest of the people of these nations and all other nations. We are confident that this book will serve as a bridge builder with new, useful, and interesting information about China, a fast-changing country.

Waitan Bund, the symbol of Shanghai, where old style buildings are mixed with Modern

Tiananmen Square (Gate of Heavenly Peace) in Beijing (Mao Zedong's picture is seen in the center). Built in 1417 in the Ming Dynasty with a total area of 440,000 square meters, Tiananmen is the largest open-urban square in the world.

1. First Steps

In China you will see people and places that are very different from what you are used to in North America or Europe. You will find China exciting, but you will have to be patient and expect a few difficulties in adjusting to this different way of life.

1.1 Money

Chinese currency is called *Renminbi* (people's money), often abbreviated as RMB. The basic unit of RMB is called the *Yuan* (¥). The official exchange rate between Yuan and US Dollars has been about 7.5 to one, although the Yuan is now pegged to a number of currencies and is partially floating. Hence the exchange rate is more variable than in the past. On the first trading day of 2008, the Yuan rose 50 points to break the 7.30 mark against the dollar.

One-yuan bills and coin.

Yuan means "round" because of the shape of Chinese coins. The Korean won and Japanese yen are cognates. One yuan is divided into 10 *jiao* and one jiao is divided into 10 *fen*. However, jiao and fen are no longer commonly used. The denominations of the *renminbi bills* now in circulation are: .1, .2, .5, and 1, 2, 5, 10, 20, 50, and 100 ¥. Coins are in denominations of .1, .5, and 1 ¥.

In the U.S., you often use your credit card or checks instead of cash. But in China, you will be using a lot of cash. Of course, your credit card is accepted when you check into a hotel (small hotels usually do not accept foreign currencies). In the U.S. the systems usually allow you to resolve money issues by yourself, but in China please do not expect the same thing to happen easily or quickly. It is always best to get a Chinese friend to help you with issues such as changing money or purchasing air or train tickets. Here are some suggestions:

- If you cannot exchange your U.S. dollars into Chinese RMB in the U.S. before you travel, do so as soon as you arrive in China.

- Do not exchange money at a street corner with a stranger. Always do so at the Bank of China or banks and hotels authorized to deal in foreign currencies and always keep your receipts, because you will need to show them when you change RMB back to your own currency at the end of your visit to China.

- If you plan to live there for a long time, open a U.S. dollar account and a Chinese RMB account so that each time you need to exchange, they will easily do it for you between your accounts.

- Do not carry a lot of cash when you go out. Nowadays you can also use your credit card or debit card to pay for hotels (usually big hotels), air tickets, and expensive items in big shopping centers. But remember that not every hotel or shopping center accepts credit or debit cards.

- Traveler's checks are the best way to carry money around in China. The exchange rate is fixed, and they can be replaced if lost or stolen. Checks can be cashed at the major branches of the Bank of China. However, this can be a time-consuming process. The Bank of China offices or currency exchange offices at airports accept traveler's checks issued by international commercial banks or traveler's check companies. Traveler's checks are accepted at some, but not all hotels and shops.

- Currency Regulations: There is no limit on the amount of foreign money that can be brought into China by tourists, but it must be declared at customs. Before you leave China you can have your RMB converted into foreign currencies at the Bank of China and obtain a valid "personal foreign exchange certificate," which verifies that the foreign currencies are obtained through authorized legal channels (the Bank of China). The certificate can be useful at customs when you leave the country.

Making tea

1.2 Tips

Do not give tips at a restaurant, because a service fee is already included in the bill. But at a large hotel in a major city, any service worker who serves you directly (except food waiters) can be tipped. You can give small tips when someone carries your baggage to your room or to your taxi when you leave the hotel. Around ten or fifteen Chinese RMB is sufficient. A small cash tip is recommended, since often a tip added to a credit card payment may not reach the service person, but be taken by the hotel.

1.3 Bargaining

Usually bargaining is not expected at a big department store, but do so when you shop from street peddlers. How to bargain? If they offer 100 RMB, you say "fifty." Then see what happens depending on the value of the items. Normally they will give you a lower price. But do not accept easily. Try to bargain more and perhaps you will get a better deal, and do not appear as if you are in a hurry to get the deal done. Sometimes, you need to walk away to get a better price. When you are on a tour with a group, usually the tour guide will take you to places for shopping, telling you these are better and inexpensive places. But it is still important to bargain in these places, because there always exists a relationship between the tour guide and the shop. If you are considering an expensive item and they want to charge you 500 RMB, you must first decide whether it is really worth the price. Then try to cut it to 100 RMB or 150 RMB to start your negotiation.

1.4 Getting Help from Your Chinese Friends

Always try to make friends from different walks of life so that you can turn to your Chinese friends for help whenever and wherever you need to. For example, have a Chinese friend from your workplace help you with issues involving changing money and the purchase of air or train tickets. For shopping, seek help from a neighbor.

Huo Guo, *the Hot Pot, is a popular dish in* Chengdu, Sichuan. *Like most of the traditional specialties from this Province,* Huo Guo *is fiery hot. At left, a fire is burning under the pot. The hot pot below is divided into two parts suggestive of the* Yin Yang *symbol: one side for very spicy food and the other for less spicy food.*

Two spicy Hot Pots, Huo Guo, *which are typical of Sichuan Provice*

1.5 Eating in China

There is an old Chinese saying: Eating well is most important for people. The Chinese have long believed that eating the right food in the right amount at the right time in the right way is good for their health and the prevention or cure of illnesses. A lot of emphasis has been placed on the link between diet and health. The Chinese traditional eating habits are still very widely accepted: to eat well for breakfast, to eat sufficiently for lunch, and to eat less for dinner. It is widely known around the world, even for many who have not been to China, that Chinese eat with chopsticks instead of knives and forks. This is because, in general, Chinese food is cut into small pieces before cooking. So at the table it is not necessary to use a knife to cut, as westerners do for their relatively large pieces of meat or vegetable.

1.6 What Do Chinese Eat?

Rice is the main staple of the people in the south, while noodles and steamed bread or steamed bun are the main diet for those living in the north. But today as living standards improve and transportation improves, people across China eat all kinds of food. A traditional Chinese breakfast consists of steamed bread or steamed bun, a bowl of rice porridge, or a bowl of bean curd milk. *Dim Sum*, originated in Guangzhou, southern China, is a unique breakfast consisting of a rich variety of steamed, baked, or fried snacks. It is also popular in other parts of China and in Chinatowns in many cities in the U.S. Chinese people eat a lot of stir-fried dishes, because the food is cooked quickly, conserving cooking oil and freshness.

1.7 Where to Eat?

Experienced travelers will tell you that you can find the best food in small or family-owned restaurants. These are not fancy-looking, but they offer unique local dishes. Of course, you may eat in the hotels, where you can also find good food, although it is not always the best. So, always have a Chinese friend suggest the best restaurants. Ask your Chinese friend to write down the names of the dishes in both Pinyin and characters so that the waiter will know exactly what you want. Also, try to find a restaurant with a lot of local customers, which means it may be really good.

1.8 Chinese Food in the U.S.

Chinese food in the U.S. has been Americanized to suit North American tastes. For example, some chefs say that they put in more sugar to suit the American taste. Moreover, restaurants use a lot of ready-made materials that do not reflect the preparation methods and real variety of Chinese cuisine. Of course, you can eat really good Chinese food in Chinatowns located in U.S. cities where the restaurants are frequented by local Chinese people. But remember, Chinese food in China is not the same as in the Chinese restaurants found in every town in the U.S.

1.9 Eating Customs and Cultural Differences

The main difference between Chinese and western eating habits is that in the West, each person has their own plate of food, but in China the dishes are placed on the table and everybody shares.

- When you are invited to eat in a restaurant by a Chinese friend, it means they will pay the bill. Chinese do not "go Dutch" as often as Americans do.

- When you eat in the home of a Chinese friend, they will certainly encourage you to eat more, picking up pieces of food with their chopsticks and placing them in your bowl or on your plate. While you are eating, your Chinese host will always say, "Help yourself. No good food to eat." This seems odd since there is plenty of good food prepared, but your host is being modest, pushing you to eat while admitting that there isn't much and it isn't good. Typically your friend will also keep encouraging you to drink more alcohol. This is a very common and polite way of treating guests in China, so your host may not notice if it makes you uncomfortable..

- Usually in the U.S., when a guest arrives, the food is already prepared, and you sit with your guest talking or sharing drinks. But in China, when you are invited to dine, you will find that your host will often leave you alone with a cup of tea, asking you to sit or watch TV while they are busy cooking in the kitchen. This may seem rude to you, making you feel uncomfortable. However, in Chinese cuisine, many good dishes need to be cooked right before they are served, to keep the best, freshest taste. Typically you will see steam coming up from the plate or bowl as it is served.

1.10 Chinese Cuisine

The Chinese have a long tradition of making excellent dishes, but the style of their Chinese cuisine varies from place to place. Traditionally, there were four major schools: *Yue* (Cantonese), *Chuan* (Sichuan), *Yang* (*Jiangsu*), *Lu* (*Shandong*). Today, many other schools of cuisine have developed across China.

Yue **Dishes** *(Yue Cai).* In Southern China, especially in *Guangdong* Province, the climate is warm and wet along the coast. All kinds of products grow throughout the year, and there is a plentiful supply of seafood and fruit. Therefore, *Yue* dishes emphasize freshness and sophistication of taste, relying less on deep-frying. In Canton you can eat all kinds of food all the year round.

Chun **Dishes** *(Chuan Cai).* In Central and Western China, chili grows very well. So, *Chuan* Dishes are known for their spiciness, especially the Hot Pot. It is so spicy and hot that it can make your tongue feel numb while tears flow from your eyes. So go to Sichuan to taste the spiciest food on Earth.

Yang **or** *Jiangsu* **Dishes** *(Su Cai or Jiangsu Cai).* The *Yang* or *Jiangsu* Cuisine is well known for its careful selection of season-based ingredients, with an emphasis on matching the colors and shapes of various dishes.

Lu **Dishes or** *Shandong* **Dishes** *(Shandong Cai).* The *Shandong* Cuisine is considered one of the most influential in Chinese cuisine. The cooking of seafood, including clams, prawns, sea cucumbers, squid, and scallops, is most characteristic of the *Lu* Cuisine. It is also unique in its wide use of its local corn, which is served as steamed or lightly fried cobs. The climate is cold in northern China and more suitable for growing wheat than rice. For this reason, *Shandong* cuisine is distinct from other schools in its use of wheat, millet, oats, and barley. These are served as porridge *(Zhou)* or in various forms of steamed and lightly fried bread. The northern cuisine is also well known for roasting meat. That is why the Beijing Roast Duck *(Beijing Kaoya)* is so popular.

Beijing is also well known for its royal cuisine. The *Shandong* school was influenced by the emperors of five dynasties who brought master chefs with them when they entered the capital city. It is said that emperors took three days to finish the legendary *Manhan* Complete Feast *(Manhan Quan Xi).*

Cooking Methods

The most common cooking methods are roasting, stir-frying, and steaming. Stir-frying, used to conserve oil and fuel, is the most popular method; its short cooking time preserves the fresh taste of the food. Steaming is often used for seafood. In the *Chaoshan* area, eastern *Guangdong* Province, a lot of seafood such as lobster, fish, shrimps, and crabs are steamed with little or no sauce. Again, the local people consider this a good way to keep the fresh seafood taste. However, deep steaming is not recommended. Normally after the water boils, around 10-18 minutes of steaming will be enough, depending on the quantity of seafood.

1.11 Names of the Dishes

The following are the names of dishes that are often seen on a Chinese menu:

Gongbao **Chicken**. This is a popular dish that originated in China's Sichuan Province. It was named after *Ding Baozhen*, the *Qing* governor of the province, who was called *Gongbao*. The official title of the *Qing* Dynasty was *Gongbao*. The dish is stir-fried with diced marinated chicken, peanuts, and red chili. It is considered a very good dish when served with rice.

Furong **Chicken or** *Furong* **Shrimp**. In the Chinese language, *furong* means "lotus." The sliced chicken or shrimp is cooked with egg white paste. The resulting pale color is that of the lotus flower.

Moo Xu **Pork**. This dish is typical of northern China. One of the main ingredients is scrambled eggs. The name of the dish comes from the yellow color of the cooked eggs. This is a strange story. Many years ago the word "egg" – *dan* in everyday language – was taboo in Beijing; it was associated with some curse words. So "egg soup" is called "Moo Shu" soup. This is because "Moo Shu" or "*Mu Xu*" is the name of the osmanthus tree in Chinese, and the color of the cooked eggs suggests the yellow-white flowers of the osmanthus tree.

The Beggar's Chicken (*Jiaohua Ji*). One day in China's *Qing* Dynasty, in what is now *Hangzhou*, in *Zhejiang* Province, a hungry beggar got a chicken. But he had no cooking tools, nor any ingredients with which to cook the chicken. It was very cold. The beggar cut down some branches from a tree and lit a fire. Then he killed the chicken, threw away its inner organs, and wrapped it with wet mud without pulling out its feathers. He threw the mud-wrapped chicken into the fire and left it for a few hours. When the fire died out, he took out the chicken and cracked open the mud. The chicken feathers came off with the hard dry mud, and a wonderful smell arose from the chicken cooked inside. It was so delicious that this way of cooking chicken spread quickly. At a later time, this cooking method was improved by adding a variety of spices and stuffing the chicken with fresh meat, shrimp, ham, and mushrooms. First the chicken was wrapped in lily leaf, and then it was sealed in mud mixed with the *Shaoxin* Wine (*Shaoxin Jiu*). These changes to the hungry beggar's method certainly improved the taste, and *Jiaohua Ji* has become a famous dish in *Hangzhou*, one of China's most famous, beautiful cities.

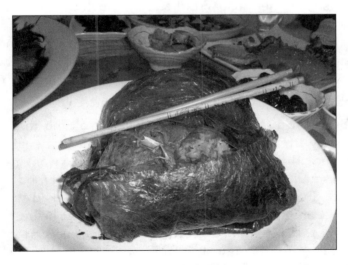

Wrapped in lily leaf, Jiaohua Ji, *the Beggar's Chicken, has been baked in a coat of mud. Stuffed and steamed, it is juicy, tender, and wonderfully aromatic.*

9

Song Zi (pine nut) Fish is sweet and sour, a traditional dish popular across China. It is made in the shape of a pine nut, Song Zi *in Chinese.*

Fried Pork Slices with Fish Taste (*Yu Xiang Rousi*). Once upon a time, in what is today China's Sichuan Province, there lived a husband and wife who were very good at cooking fish. They used a variety of ingredients such as green onion, ginger, garlic, vinegar, soy sauce, and wine. One evening, hoping to save for herself the next day the leftovers from a fish, the wife put them all into dish of pork. Then her husband came back and he was hungry. She was afraid that the pork might be nasty, but her husband liked it so much that he asked her how she had made it. She told him, with hesitation, for fear he would be angry, but he said that the dish was wonderful and encouraged her to do it again. Now this strange method of cooking pork slices with fish is popular throughout China and overseas in Chinese restaurants.

Ma Po **Bean Curd (*Ma Po Doufu*).** Once upon a time, in the *Qing* Dynasty, in *Chengdu,* which is now the capital city of Sichuan Province, there was a woman whose last name was Chen. She ran a small restaurant that was famous for good food at good prices. Everyone called her *Ma Po,* "pockmarked woman," because she had many pockmarks on her face. At her restaurant, her specialty was a bean curd dish that was very spicy – hot and tasty. To distinguish it from other bean curd dishes in other restaurants, her customers called her special bean curd *Ma Po* Bean Curd (*Ma Po Doufu*).

10

1.12 Driving

Nowadays you are able to change your international driver's license into a Chinese license after you take certain tests. However, driving in China can be challenging to a foreigner who is not familiar with the Chinese concept of traffic safety. China has been a kingdom of bicycles for a long time, so bicyclists and even pedestrians struggle with automobiles for space in the streets. You need very good skills to take part in this struggle.

A kingdom of bicycles

At present a foreign or international driver's license is not recognized in China. But you may change it into a Chinese driver's license and drive in China. To do this you need to:

- have lived overseas for a consecutive period of 6 months with a valid foreign license or international driving license.

- have a health checkup and present your passport or Chinese Temporary Resident Card at the Chinese Motor Vehicle Authority (MVA).

- have your foreign or international driver's license translated into Chinese. The translation must bear the signature of the translator and the seal of the translator's work unit or organization.

- present your foreign or international driver's license and a photocopy, which will be kept by the Chinese MVA.

- pass a written and road test. Those with more than three years driving experience overseas are exempt from the road test.

As China's auto industry has developed rapidly in the past 20 years, and as its people have earned more money, many citizens have been able to buy cars, especially in metropolitan areas. However, it takes time to build highways that meet international standards and for people's understanding of traffic rules to catch up. In the bumper-to-bumper rush hour in a big city, the best way to travel is not by car but by bus or taxi. So, the best advice is this: Don't drive in China. If you live on a campus or in an apartment, it is a good idea to ride a bicycle for short errands.

1.13 Air travel

In the U.S., you may just pick up the phone or go online and get your air ticket in a matter of minutes. In China, people usually go to the booking office personally to reserve and buy a ticket. If you are with an organization or company, ask them to make the reservation for you. It would be much easier than doing it yourself. Or get a Chinese friend to accompany you to the booking office. During traditional festivals or China's one-week national holiday travel peaks, tickets can be harder to get and more expensive than usual. So always reserve your tickets early. Always reserve a taxi for your travel to the airport or get your organization to drive you there. Getting to the airport through big city traffic jams could cost you hours. It wouldn't hurt to start for the airport as early as possible, much earlier than you would in your own country.

1.14 Traveling by Train/Bus

In the U.S. you can pick up a phone and reserve your train ticket days, weeks, or even months in advance. This is not true in China, where you normally reserve your ticket a few days in advance. In many small places, you have to line up to buy your ticket for today's or tomorrow's train/bus. It can be very frustrating during holidays when you find it hard to get a ticket for your trip or buy a return ticket. So when you decide to travel by train/bus, always get a Chinese friend or your sponsoring organization to help you get the ticket. If you cannot get a sleeper seat on a train you will sit in a very crowded train. How crowded can it be during holidays? The answer is SEEING IS BELIEVING! It is often through your experience of taking a train/bus that you will really understand why China has been adopting population control policies. But the train/bus is the place where you can see the real China. Food is served on the train, but it is usually expensive. It is a good idea to buy some food or snacks and drinking water before you get on the train/bus.

1.15 Hotels

Where to stay

Today in China's big cities or popular scenic spots, you can easily find expensive four- or five-star international hotels. But many foreigners prefer to stay in two- or three-star regular hotels with good prices, close to the airport or train station. To decide which hotel to stay in, you have to consider the distance factor. If it is far from the airport or train station, it can take longer than expected to get there. In the three Golden Week Periods: the Spring Festival (Chinese New Year), May 1st (Labor Day), and October 1st (National Day), all Chinese have a one-week holiday, and hotel prices in some popular touristic spots can be very high. On the other hand, in some cities hotel prices may drop because many people are away on a vacation.

Most universities and colleges have their own hostels or hotels. These can be very good in price and service. When they travel in China, a lot of foreign students and teachers stay there. If you are traveling on business, it is a good idea to ask your client or your contact to make reservations for you.

How to find hotels and make reservations

How to locate an ideal one? It is very easy to get on the website and search and make your reservation. Credit cards are accepted. From the following four websites you can get hotel information for China's major cities:

www.asiarooms.com/china/index.html
www.china-hotels.com
www.shanghaihotels.co
www.bjhotels.com/english/index.htm

Always ask your friends/colleagues if they know some good hotels in the place you are going to. They might help you to reserve your room more easily because you may have language barriers when you communicate with hotel staff, especially in small cities and remote places. You are advised to make your reservation early, about 7-10 days before your trip.

*A Chinese style country inn with blankets folded
on the beds in the typical Chinese fashion*

Facilities and service

Hotel rooms are normally equipped with a telephone, TV, internet connection, hair dryer, iron, and refrigerator. You will be provided with towels, toothpaste, toothbrush, soap, shampoo, and a comb. Breakfast is not included. We don't give tips in the hotel, but many foreigners give small tips to those who help them carry their luggage to their room when they check in. There are no tips

14

for the waiters/waitresses and the taxi driver, because a service fee is charged already. If you receive very good service and want to express your appreciation, you may write a brief comment in their Customer Comment Book, and they will certainly enjoy reading it.

1.16 Traveling by Bicycle

Although more and more Chinese people have private cars, most people still rely on bicycles as a daily commuting tool or for shopping and just getting around. Most places have special lanes for cyclists on the streets. You are not allowed to ride your bike on the sidewalk. Also, you can put a basket on the back of your bike for your own belongings. You do not have to wear a helmet when cycling. Remember to lock your bicycle. In many places, especially in small towns, cyclists, pedestrians, and automobiles travel on the same streets. For your own safety, try to avoid riding your bicycle in such an environment.

1.17 Health and Medical Care

Although China has made tremendous progress in its economic reforms, its reform in health care has not been successful. According to China's official *Xinhua* News Agency (12/15/2005), about 50% of the rural population and 70% of the urban population are not covered by any medical insurance. More than half of the medical costs are paid out of the pockets of the patients, rather than by national or private health insurance. In 2003, the United Nations ranked China 61st among the 192 UN countries in insured citizenry.

Before China started its economic reforms and opened to the rest of the world, medical care was provided free by the state. But this "iron bowl" has been broken in the wake of economic reforms, and employees have been asked to pay a portion of their medical expenses. Those companies that are rich can offer good health care for their employees, but a lot of enterprises are not able to pay medical expenses for their employees. Besides, the prices of medicine and hospital services have skyrocketed. Many cannot afford to see doctors. Since 2000, China has initiated a cooperative health care system in limited rural areas where the state, the local government, and the citizen share health care expenses.

Experience in the past two decades has shown China that its health care reforms cannot just rely on the market. The government must play a bigger role. According to the World Health Organization, the per capita government spending in the U.S. on health care was $2,368 in 2003 but in China it was just $33. While China's economic advances are often in the world media headlines today, its effort to reform its health care system and its problems in this aspect are under-reported. China is now facing a variety of medical challenges, including an AIDS epidemic and the newly-emerging disease SARS.

Hospital service for foreigners

Normally, for those from abroad who are teaching or working in China, their employment contracts have already specified that the school or enterprise would cover the medical cost when the foreigner is sick. But this does not include what is known in America as a free annual medical check-up. Nor does the contract usually say what is the maximum expense the Chinese employer would cover. Make sure you note the relevant stipulations in your contract with your potential Chinese employer. Nowadays some big companies in China are starting to buy medical insurance for their overseas employees.

Usually when a foreigner is sick, they get treated, and the Chinese employer covers the normal expenses. But if you have a serious illness requiring a hospital stay, and you are not sure what's wrong, you are advised to go back to your home country for thorough testing and treatment.

Hospitals

Hospital service, including emergency ambulance service, is easily accessible in cities. Advanced medical equipment like that in the U.S. and Canada can also be found in good hospitals in China. Colleges and universities have their own clinics/hospitals where you get normal non-emergency treatment. The school doctors will send you to hospitals outside of school if they are unable to treat you. Usually the foreign affairs office of your school will assign someone to accompany you to the hospital so that you will not have language problems when you are in the hospital. For an emergency, the number for ambulance service is 112.

Pharmacy

You are advised to take your daily medicine or vitamin supplements with you to China. If you work at a school or company, you can get medicine from your workplace, so you do not usually need to buy your medicine in a pharmacy. Medicine, including antibiotics and traditional Chinese medicine, can easily be purchased from a pharmacy or a department store without a doctor's prescription. Nevertheless, if you do need to go to a pharmacy, make sure you have your doctor's written prescription (permission). This is not just for your own safety but also for your convenience in reimbursement. Always get a Chinese colleague or friend to accompany you to a pharmacy, because of the language barriers you might encounter.

1.18 Communication

Post offices

Throughout China, post offices are accessible, and in general the services are reliable. It takes about 9-14 days for regular first-class airmail to arrive in China from the U.S. and vice versa. Express mail takes about five days, though sometimes it can be quicker depending on the location. If you are near Beijing or Shanghai where there are direct flights to the U.S., the mail can arrive sooner. For letters and packages, Priority mail from the U.S. is a good option and less expensive than Express. Sending a parcel by ship from China is cheaper but can take as long as 2-3 months. It is no longer possible to send surface mail from the U.S. via the post office.

Telecommunications

Since China opened its doors to the outside in 1979, its tele-communications industry has developed enormously, with 372 million main telephone lines in use and 515 million mobile cellular phones in use in August 2007. By mid-2007 there were 162 million internet users in China, the second largest internet user after the U.S. In major tourist spots across the country internet is accessible. In addition to hotels, internet cafes host many foreign tourists. It is also very easy to use fax machines.

It is much more expensive to call from China to the U.S. than from the U.S. to China. A lot of foreigners save money by using a Chinese phone card to call their home in the U.S. or Canada only to ask their families and friends to call back. Also, if you dial someone's cell phone number in China from the U.S., the cell phone user in China will also be charged and it is more expensive. So, if it is not an emergency, you are advised to dial landline numbers in China.

Calling inside China

To use a landline phone to call another landline phone number in another city inside China, dial 0 followed by the area code of the other city and the phone number of the person you are calling. If it is within the same city, you do not dial 0. To call a cell phone number, dial the cell phone number directly without 0.

Calling China from the U.S. and Canada

To call a landline phone from the U.S., dial 011 followed by China's country code 86 and the area code and number of the person you are calling. To call a cell phone number in China, dial 011+86+cell phone number.

Using a phone card to call China from the U.S.

Using a phone card to call China from America, you need to dial the access number followed by the PIN provided by the phone card company. If the China number is 0754 (area code)-123456, you

18

need to dial 011-86-754-123456. Note that the 0 before 754 should be omitted. Also, you need to know that China is 13 hours ahead of New York in the winter (standard time) and 12 hours ahead in the summer with daylight saving time. In June, if it is 8 a.m. in New York, it is 8 p.m. in China.

Useful numbers

Emergency Phone Numbers: Crime: 110, Ambulance: 112, Fire: 119

To find a number by using business and organization names anywhere in China, dial 114.

Using email in China

If you have an employer, ask them to set up an internal email account for you so that you can connect with your colleagues and classmates. You will find it very easy to get access to a computer. You may use your existing email account (Yahoo, Hotmail, etc.).

1.19 Electricity

In China 220 voltage is used for electric appliances (in the U.S. 110 voltage is used). If you take an appliance bought in America to China, you need to buy a converter in the U.S. Also, you need to buy a plug in the U.S. that can fit into the outlet in China so that you can plug in your converter to transfer the voltage. A lot of digital cameras and other electronic devices purchased in the U.S. have battery chargers or adapters designed for both 110 and 220 voltages, so you do not need to buy a converter to use them.

Actually, today many electric appliances available in the U.S. or Canada are made in China. You can buy exactly the same devices in China at similar or cheaper prices. China has changed. Twenty or thirty years ago many Chinese people returning home from abroad brought electronic appliances. Today no one wants to do this. Now what they bring back to China are mostly health products, such as vitamin supplements, or cosmetics, such as famous brand perfumes and facial creams.

Da Yan Pagoda, located in Xian, Shannxi Province, was built in the year 652, over 1,300 years ago, to collect Buddhist works from India. It is a holy place for Buddhists.

1.20 U.S. and Canadian Embassies and Consulates in China

The address for the U.S. Embassy in Beijing is:

U.S. Embassy in China
3 Xiu Shui Bei Jie
Beijing 100600, China
Tel: (86-10) 6532-3831
After hours/Emergencies: (86-10) 6532-1910
Fax: (86-10) 6532-4153, 6532-3178
Website: www.usembassy-china.org.cn

There are five consulates, located in Chengdu, Guangzhou, Shanghai, Shenyang, and Hong Kong. For addresses see Appendix A, page 76.

The Embassy of Canada to China
19 Dong Zhi Men Wai Street, Chaoyang District
Beijing 100600, China
Tel: (86-10) 6532-3536
Fax: (86-10) 6532-4072
E-mail: infocentrechina@international.gc.ca
Website: www.china.gc.ca

There are three Canadian consulates in Guangzhou, Shanghai, and Chongqing. For addresses see Appendix A, page 78.

1.21 Weights and Measurements

The metric system is used in China in weights and measurements. Chinese people also still use their traditional system. The following is a conversion table.

Length	Metric	Traditional Chinese	U.S.
	1 km	2 *li*	0.62 mile
	1.607 km	3.218 *li*	1 mile
	1 m	3 *chi*	3.281 feet
	0.305 m	0.915 *chi*	1 foot
Weight	Metric	Tr. Chinese	U.S.
	1 kg	2 *jin*	2.205 pounds
	0.454 kg	.908 *jin*	1 pound
Area	Metric	Tr. Chinese	U.S.
	1 hectare (ha)	15 *mu*	2.47 acres
	0.067 hectare	1 *mu*	0.165 acre
	0.405 hectare	6.08 *mu*	1 acre
	Metric	Tr. Chinese	U.S.
Volume	1 liter	1 *sheng*	0.22 gallon
	4.546 liters	4.546 *sheng*	1 gallon

2. Philosophical Concepts, Culture, and Manners

2.1 Philosophical Bases of Chinese Culture: Confucianism and Taoism

In China, while having an impact on people's life, religions have not become institutionalized as in the West. What orients people's thinking and behavior are the philosophical ideas that have been deeply rooted in the hearts and minds of the Chinese people for thousands of years. The most important philosophical bases of Chinese culture are Confucianism and Taoism.

Confucianism

Confucianism is based on the teachings and writings of the Chinese philosopher Confucius, who lived in the 6th and 5th centuries B.C.E. Confucius prescribed an ideal society where individuals relate to one another according to fixed roles and where **hierarchy** is given great importance. The basic values are *jen* (benevolence), *shu* (reciprocity), *yi* (righteousness), and *li* (enactment of rituals). Elders are to be respected and the young to be protected. Children should not go far away while the parents are still alive. The children must obey the father; the wife must obey the husband; the younger brother obeys the older brother. The rulers should exercise benevolence to those ruled and those ruled should show obedience to the rulers. An ideal society will be built when everyone understands their role and obligations to others and when social structures are adhered to.

Confucianism is an ethical system that seeks to teach the proper way for all people to behave in society. Each **relationship**, husband-

22

Confucius, still influential after 2500 years.

wife, parents-children, and ruler-subjects, involves a set of obligations which, if upheld, would lead to a just and harmonious society. Following Confucius' teachings would also promote a stable, lasting government. It was not until the Han Dynasty (221 B.C.E.) that Confucianism was adopted by the emperor. It soon became the official philosophy of the country.

These philosophical concepts explain, perhaps, why Chinese society changed so slowly in the past and why China has a deeply rooted relationship-oriented (*Guanxi*) culture. In China everything seems to be determined by how well you relate to people who could help you succeed or help you out during difficult times. Life will be much easier if you have friends in China who have good relations with people in different circles. It will help you find business partners; and you need friends in China so that when the need arises they can help you a lot, even if only to buy a train ticket or change money. On the negative side, this *Guanxi*-oriented culture has led to over-reliance on friends rather than self-effort, and it has even led to corruption.

Confucianism and China today

Today in China, people are still encouraged to show respect to the elderly and take care of the younger generation. But with the opening to the outside world and consequent reform of the rigid socialist planned economy to a more open market-oriented economy, the Chinese are motivated to implement faster changes in their life. Leaders at different levels are still respected by subordinates, but there are now less rigid and more cordial relationships, and a relaxed informality can be seen today at various levels of leadership.

Equality and democracy are being promoted in some organizations, and in many places people are welcome to express their own ideas and criticism toward the leadership. Reliance on relationships to climb to a higher position and the occasional resulting corruption are being condemned in China today. People are encouraged to rely on their own efforts to succeed in society. More and more corrupt officials have been brought to justice.

While the traditional culture is still deeply rooted in China, western culture including music, food, and the arts has been allowed to enter China so that people have more choices. China is engaged with the rest of the world and is developing a new culture of its own. It is very different from that of any other country. Will democracy take root in China? Probably, but it will take time to grow, to mature. Will it be like that of the western world? Perhaps, but more likely it will not be wholly western. It may be transformed, Chinese style.

Taoism

Taoism is both a philosophy and a religion. The founder was *Laozi* (Lao-tze). *Dao* (Tao) literally means "the way" or "the path." It is the source of all existence, and it reveals deep connections between humanity and nature. It derives primarily from the *Dao De Jing* (道德经), which claims that an ever-changing universe follows the Tao, the path. The Yin-Yang is the symbol of Taoism. The universe is explained by the theories of opposites. Everything in the universe, including the human body, is composed of two opposing elements in mutual interaction: Yin and Yang, heaven and earth, male and female, outer strength and inner strength, light and darkness, etc. When the two elements are in balance or in harmony problems will be resolved. Man must be in harmony with nature.

Different from religions, Taoism is not about deities and beliefs; it is a philosophy about the self. Taoists believe in their

24

own worth and in leading a life of balance and harmony. This ancient philosophy directs Chinese thinking to this day. The people of China have been and are encouraged to be in harmony within the family, with their neighbors, and with foreign countries. The theme of harmony is much emphasized by the Chinese government in its policies within China and in its diplomatic relations with other countries.

Feng Shui

Feng Shui means wind and water. It is a system of theories and methods that originated from the concept of Yin-Yang and understanding the five elements of nature. It is used in the selection of houses, buildings, and tombs. Some Chinese, especially those living in South China and overseas, believe that they experience the influence of nature, negative or positive, while staying anywhere. Choosing the right location to live and work and to own property has a crucial impact on their fortunes. *Feng Shui* has a long history with a lot of interpretations. Some regard it as an integrated science of the environment, geography, architecture, and health. Others think it is just a superstition. The main ideas are that our surroundings change our emotions, moods, health, and even our fate, family relations, and careers. It is vital to be in harmony with nature. Some people spend a lot of money hiring a *Feng Shui* master to help them select a new house or building or to give them suggestions of ways to adjust these places so that the people using them will have a brighter future.

2.2 Chinese Manners

Although China is a unified nation with a common language – *Putonghua* (Mandarin) – there are 56 ethnic groups. Each ethnic group has its own history and culture, and their beliefs and values are still deeply rooted in every part of their daily life. While each ethnic group has its own unique way of life, some general cultural patterns prevail in most parts of the country.

Table manners

Chinese pay a lot of attention to how they eat at the table. While table manners may vary from place to place, the following are common ones:

- Do not just take any chair to sit down at the dinner table. Wait till the host gives you a position to sit at the table.

- When exchanging business cards, hold yours with two hands and let your title face the receiver.

- When a toast is proposed for you, drink it up and show to your host that the cup is empty to show respect.

- Before you move the revolving table with different dishes, make sure no one else is getting food from the plates on the table.

- Do not stick two chopsticks upright in your bowl of rice. It is a big taboo because the shrine for the dead has a bowl of rice with two sticks of incense stuck straight.

- Chinese like to use toothpicks at the end of a meal to clean their teeth. If you feel a need to do so, try to cover your mouth with both hands while doing it. Then put the toothpick down discreetly.

- To show their hospitality, many Chinese hosts like to pick up the good food with their own chopsticks and put it onto your plate. When this happens, try to eat it and say how good the food is. If you cannot eat so much or do not feel comfortable, just thank the host and leave the food there.

- Do not tap on your bowl with the chopsticks, because beggars used to do it.

- When your host pours tea or wine into your cup or glass, tap the table gently with your hand to show "Thanks." (This is a widespread practice in southern China.)

- If you are a host, offer the seat facing the door to your most senior or distinguished guest. Make sure the teapot spout does not point at anybody.

26

Hugging

Do they hug? Not in the past. But today with the opening to the outside world, you might see young people in big cities, especially teenagers or college students, hug on some occasions, such as meeting family members or friends they have not seen for a long time. They may also hug upon saying farewell or congratulating friends.

Handshaking

Handshaking is the most commonly accepted practice across ages and regions. Sometimes you might feel that your Chinese friend's enthusiastic handshake is overly firm.

Bowing

You might have the impression of Chinese putting both hands before their chests to show respect to their parents, grandparents, senior citizens, and superiors or VIP's. That was a custom a long time ago. Today, during the Chinese New Year or Spring Festival, in some places, you can still see some people doing this.

Loud voice

Very often when you hear Chinese talking they seem to be arguing. Actually, they are not. In many places people speak loudly to express their emotions, especially their excitement. Their voices may sound very loud to you because their language is tonal with four different tones and the fourth tone, which is a strong falling tone, is unusually loud.

2.3 Common Ways of Greeting and Answering Greetings

For a lot of people today, nodding is a common way of greeting others, especially among friends or those close to each other. In many places, you are often asked, "Have you eaten?" or "Where are you going?" (in a nice way). Do not feel odd or feel that you are going to be followed. These two expressions are just polite daily greetings like "How's it going?" in the U.S. – a common greeting, not a real question or an invitation. Then how to answer when greeted with these two questions? Just tell the truth: whether you have eaten or not and where you are going, followed by "and you?" Please refer to Chapter 7 for a list of daily expressions in Chinese Pinyin (Romanization) and characters and an English translation.

2.4 Responding to Compliments

It is customary for many Chinese to sound humble as if they are not worthy of the praise when you congratulate them on achievements or compliment them on a beautiful dress. This is a significant cultural difference. In the U.S. when this happens, you usually say, "Thanks." But a Chinese might say " No. I'm not good enough. It's far from being perfect." or "Oh, this is an ordinary dress that only costs 40 RMB." But they don't mean that what they have accomplished is not good. It is just their usual way of responding to compliments like this.

2.5 Common Ways of Expressing Gratitude and Replies to Gratitude

The most common polite expressions, *xiexie* (Thank you) and *qing* (Please), are used much less often in China than in western countries. For a little favor like borrowing a dictionary, opening a door for someone, passing something to the people at table, etc. such polite expressions are often omitted and regarded as unnecessary, especially among friends and family members. Chinese people think that appreciation is understood and need not be expressed, which is sometimes considered rudeness or lack of consideration by westerners. The most common replies to "thank you" are *bu yong xie* (you're welcome), or *bu keqi* (don't mention it).

2.6 Smiling Apology

When Chinese people make a mistake or do something wrong, they apologize by saying "I am sorry." Sometimes, Chinese people make apologies with a smile. By doing so, this adds a gesture of humility and even embarrassment to the apology! To an American, this smile may indicate a lack of sincerity or even be a sign of disrespect, adding to the offense instead of making a sincere apology. If you receive a smiling Chinese apology for a mistake committed, either involving work or something else, it's best just to say, "Okay, no problem now," and part by shaking hands and letting the person know that you have accepted their apology.

2.7 Taking Photos

It is very interesting to notice that in recent years many Chinese people when communicating with foreign friends or business partners like to take pictures with them. For many, such pictures mean a lot to them because they can show to their friends or relatives that they have friends or business partners abroad. So, whenever you can, offer your Chinese friends an opportunity to take a picture with them. They will consider it a very nice gesture. And they usually show great interest when you show them the pictures of your family members and describe them. So, before your trip to China you might prepare a few pictures of your family members or your house or places of interest.

2.8 Gift Giving

Once upon a time, a man went on a long journey to see his friend, with a swan as a gift. But it flew out of the cage on his way. He tried to catch it but what he got was only a feather. Yet, he continued his journey with the feather. When his friend received this unexpected gift, he was deeply moved. So Chinese have a popular saying: The gift is not as much as the thought behind it. Unfortunately, this is an old story now. Some Chinese think it's insulting to be given a cheap gift. A cheap gift is considered embarrassing and disgraceful even if it was hard to get.

2.9 Taboos in Gift-giving

China is a nation of ritual. Gift-giving is a part of life as it is everywhere in the world. The following Chinese cultural rituals merit attention:

- Do not give a clock as a gift because the pronunciation of the word "clock, " 送钟Song Zhong sounds like attending a funeral, 送终 Song Zhong.

- Do not send pears as gift because "pears" (梨) sounds like "separation" (离) in Chinese.

- Do not use black and white paper to wrap your gifts, because these two colors are often associated with death.

2.10 Culture Bumps

Contact with people from another culture, whether in your own country or abroad, inevitably produces surprises – some pleasant, some not. These result from differences, particularly in language, values, and behaviors. Although we know other cultures are different, it is another thing to experience and to deal with the differences. While it is easy to accept pleasant surprises, the same is not true for unpleasant ones. The differences that cause irritations ranging from minor to serious are called "culture bumps."

In China, culture bumps may occur in a number of areas. Clearly, the more you know about the local culture, the less likely you are to be in conflict with it or "bumped" by it. However, if you are new to the culture, it is best to anticipate that problems will arise. These can range from simple matters of daily life, such as how to walk down a busy street, to more important matters such as gender relations.

Coping with these culture bumps is part of living in China, and in the experience of coping you will have opportunities to learn about both Chinese culture and your own. This is one of the reasons the intercultural experience usually results in deepening your self-awareness while you are also developing new knowledge, skills, and attitudes (hopefully positive ones).

Culture bumps can vary widely depending on the size of the city or the region in China. Large cities and many fast-developing areas seem as sophisticated as any North American city, while less-developed places might cause more culture bumps. Many North Americans have cited as personal culture bumps things like these:

The noise level: Chinese generally tolerate more noise than North Americans. For example, in some less-developed places it is not unusual for drivers to use their horns a lot, for loudspeakers to be really loud (even on public buses), for people to talk during concerts and movies, and for children to be allowed to scream and be active in public places. Chinese parents are especially tolerant of their children's behavior. They will talk quietly to the children to correct them.

Another distinctive feature about noise is what happens at the dinner table. It is commonly accepted that both hosts and guests talk loudly over meals. The more heated talk they have, the happier and more relaxed they are.

Pollution: Air, water, and environmental degradation are problems in China. For cold drinks, water from the tap is not as drinkable as it is in North America; first it must be boiled. In offices and at home, Chinese drink either bottled or boiled water. Depending upon the size of the city (or quality of the hotel), water for consumption should be considered carefully. Boiled water in thermoses has been the norm in the past. Bottled water and well-known bottled drinks should be a standard item for daily use.

Air in many large cities contains more dust and coal particles than air in North America. Travelers to China who have a history of breathing problems should consult with their physician about protection or mitigation of air pollution ailments. Face masks, inhalers, and medicines should be considered by those susceptible to breathing problems such as chronic bronchitis or asthma.

In some streets in less-developed areas, as you get farther from large metropolitan areas, litter, trash disposal, and human waste disposal becomes more problematic. Certain streets may be designated for waste disposal bins. This means that litter, including human waste (delivered each morning by chamber pots) is collected on these streets.

The Eastern toilet: These are wide, ceramic-rimmed slits in the floor, requiring the users to squat over the slit in order to relieve themselves. While more and more homes and public places have replaced the eastern toilet with western toilets like those used in North America and Europe, in many places you will still find the eastern toilets in older hotels, public restrooms, schools, trains, and older private homes. This can be especially difficult for Westerners as there is usually no grab bar. It is also advisable to carry a supply of Kleenex-type tissues or toilet paper, and a small bottle of hand sanitizer or packaged hand wipes. This may be your most difficult culture bump.

Lack of rest stops and toilet facilities: To travel in China, it is most important to use the airport or hotel facilities before leaving on a trip. There is a lack of clean facilities on trips, especially in less-developed areas. Again, no one will come to your rescue with toilet tissue. So be prepared!

Smoking: In North America, smoking is not allowed in many public places, such as restaurants and waiting rooms at airports and train stations. In China, it is common to see people smoke in those and other places, even in places with NO SMOKING signs.

In many places, offering cigarettes may still be a gesture of courtesy. As a guest you might find people asking you "Do you like a cigarette?" as they take out a pack of cigarettes. If you do not smoke you may feel uncomfortable turning them down, but you can just say, "I do not smoke, thanks." They will understand.

Traffic on the streets of Shanghai

Walking down the street: While driving or walking, Chinese stick to the right-hand side of the street. Despite the established rules, some Chinese don't follow any pattern while walking. People walk on either side of streets or sidewalks in either direction, and there is no tradition of passing people you meet on the left or right when walking. You also have to keep your eyes open for hazards in streets and on sidewalks. If you aren't careful, you may step into a missing grate, a hole, or a vendor's stand.

The need to please: In general, Chinese people are hospitable to foreigners. It's difficult for them to say 'No' to a foreign friend. When they find something that is difficult to do or to answer, they usually say 'No' in a roundabout way rather than making a direct negative reply. For example, if you say you would like to go to the park or some tourist attraction, your friend will say they would love to take you – and they really would, although they know they probably can't. They just don't want to disappoint you by saying they can't.

Cleaning up: Chinese homes are generally very neat and clean and well organized. However, in some areas – outside the home, in the garden, or in the street – the picture is different. Some Chinese are unconcerned about littering. North Americans and Europeans who feel strongly about picking up litter find this difficult to adjust to. In fast food establishments, North Americans are likely to "bus" their own tables. This is not the case in China.

National pride: Chinese are often nationalistic and quite proud of their country, as we are of ours. Today, China is probably the number two superpower in the world and the Chinese know it. They are especially sensitive to the notion that Taiwan is a separate nation. They consider her to be part of China. Any discussion or acknowledgement of Taiwan can be a sensitive issue and is best avoided.

Use of public space: Chinese typically make themselves at home in public places. People will sit or squat down on curbs and sidewalks or in entryways, and one often sees people taking naps in parks or any green space.

Resting in public by the side of a road

Power and privilege: Nowadays, Chinese are more comfortable showing their financial, social, and political status. For example, they may quite openly use their status or personal connections to obtain personal favors or exemptions.

Getting change for big bills: This may not be common, yet sometimes it happens. You may end up paying too much unless you carry small bills. For example, taxi drivers often can't or won't make change, and shop owners commonly decline to change a big bill for you unless you are buying something. Carefully examine items before you purchase them, because it is unusual for store owners to take things back. You will notice that most stores have a machine that checks the bills for counterfeit money.

Most of these examples seem quite innocuous when read, but they can be irritating when experienced. You expect simple things to happen the way they do in your home country. When they don't, the normal reaction is to get mad at an individual or to be annoyed at the culture. The trick to avoiding this negative experience is to know what your Chinese host would expect in the Chinese situation. You can't avoid the culture bumps; they are part of any intercultural experience. However, knowing about them ahead of time will help you anticipate and avoid the pain, and it may also make you more open to discovering other culture bumps of your own once you are in China. How you deal with them will serve as an indicator of your level of adjustment. You must make your own decisions about whether to be annoyed or to accept the difference between your way and the new way – the Chinese way.

3. Country Facts

3.1 Geography and Climate

Location

Continental United States and China, located in the east of Asia, are almost exactly opposite each other on the planet. Until recent times, travel, trade, and exchange between the two countries was limited by the great distances involved. With the advent of air travel, distances have been shortened, so that today traveling east across the Pacific Ocean from Shanghai, China, takes about 11 hours nonstop to San Francisco. A direct flight from Shanghai to New York takes 14 hours. Now there are 13 daily flights between the U.S. and China.

Land

China has an area of 9,600,000 square kilometers. When northern China is covered with snow, and people are skiing, *Shantou*, on the southern coast of China, is enjoying the spring season, and the villagers in the south are doing their spring plowing. When eastern China is covered with morning sunshine, the far west of the country is still in the dark. This very large country borders on 14 other countries and possesses many islands scattered across its territorial waters. The largest is Taiwan and the second largest is Hainan.

China is slightly larger than the U.S. including Alaska. It is the third-largest country in the world next to Russia and Canada. Despite China's large area, its farmland makes up only seven percent of the world total. China is experiencing a severe shortage of farmland, especially with the urbanization brought about by rapid economic development. More than sixty percent of its population lives on the plains and basins that make up less than one-third of the country's territory. Mountain areas make up one third of the area; one quarter is plateau, and hills are about ten percent. China's population is largely concentrated on the more developed eastern part, but now the Chinese government is encouraging economic development in the west.

Rivers

The *Chiang Jiang* (*Yangtze* River), is the longest river in China, and the third-longest in the world, after the Nile in Africa and the Amazon in South America. With a humid, warm climate, a lot of rainfall, and fertile soil, the region of the middle and lower *Chiang Jiang* is an important agricultural region with a natural transportation artery linking west and east. The second largest river is the *Huang He* (Yellow River). The *Huang He* valley is considered the cradle of ancient Chinese civilization. China also has a famous man-made river—the Grand Canal, running from *Beijing* in the north to *Hangzhou* in the south. The construction of this man-made canal started as early as the fifth century B.C.E. It is the oldest and longest man-made canal in the world.

Land forms

Mountains, hills, and plateaus make up over sixty percent of China's total territory. The most well-known mountains in China include the world's highest mountain, Mount *Qomolangma* in Tibet, *Changbai Shan* in the northeast, *Wutai Shan* in *Shanxi* Province, *Tai Shan* in *Shandong* Province, *Hua Shan* in *Shaanxi* Province, *Huang Shan* in *Anhui* Province, *Lu Shan* in *Jiangxi* Province, *Emei Shan* in *Sichuan* Province, *Wuyi Shan* in *Fujian* Province, and *Yu Shan* in *Taiwan* Province. *Huang Shan* in *Anhui* is generally considered the most beautiful.

Huang Shan in the south of Anhui Province

Mineral resources

China possesses over 150 different minerals. The following are among the world's largest deposits: coal, iron, copper, aluminum,

The waterfalls and river at Jiuzhaigou

antimony, molybdenum, manganese, tin, lead, zinc, and mercury. The coal reserves are mainly found in the north, northeast, and southwest. China is also very rich in petroleum, natural gas, oil shale, phosphorus, and sulfur. Petroleum reserves are mainly located in the north, northeast, northwest, and in the continental shelves of east China.

Climate and temperature

The Old Summer Palace in the snow

China is situated in the northern temperate zone. Its climate is affected by the monsoon that blows from Siberia and the Mongolia Plateau each year from September and October to March and April. The monsoon decreases as it goes southward, resulting in dry and cold winters. It blows into China from the ocean in the summer, causing a lot of rain. The difference in temperature between the north and south can be as huge as forty degrees Celsius. In the winter in the north, snow covers everything, yet in *Hainan* or *Shantou* in the south, there is no snow at all. The *Qinghai*-Tibet Plateau is covered by snow all the year round, while the southern *Yunnan-Guizhou* Plateau has spring weather in almost every season. *Kunming*, the capital of *Yunnan* Province, is called the Spring City. But in eastern China, especially the *Huaihe* River Valley, there is a clear pattern of the four seasons: spring, summer, autumn, and winter.

When you travel in China during the summer, especially to the mountain areas, be careful of the big drop in the temperature in the evening. Always bring your jacket, woolen sweater, or even heavy clothing if you climb the high mountains. Celsius is used in China. Here is the conversion formula:

Fahrenheit = (1.8 x Celsius) + 32
Celsius = (Fahrenheit − 32) ÷ 1.8

3.2 Population, Religions, and Holidays

Ethnic groups

China is a multi-ethnic country with 56 ethnic groups. The Han people make up over 93.3 percent of the total population, concentrated in forty percent of the country's total area. The rest of the 55 ethnic groups, called minority nationalities, inhabit sixty percent of the total territory, mainly in the border areas. Each has its own unique culture and customs deeply rooted in daily life.

All ethnic groups enjoy equal rights by China's Constitution. Regardless of the size of its population, each minority group is also represented in the National People's Congress, which is the highest legislative power in China. There are five national autonomous regions and 75 autonomous counties administering their own local affairs. Since the country opened its door to the outside world and implemented reforms, the Chinese government has been giving more support and preferential treatment to the less developed minority regions to help them develop their economy and improve their living standards.

Population

China has a population of 1.3 billion, the world's largest, concentrated in the east of the country. Fewer people live in the west. The national average density of population is 119 per square kilometer. The average size of household was 3.7 persons. The average life-span in China is 70.8 years (73.40 years for females and 68.71 for males).

If you go to China and sit or stand in a crowded train or bus, you will certainly better understand why the Chinese government has been carrying out the one-couple-one-child policy for the past thirty years. In cities, a couple is allowed to have one child. Those who live in rural areas can have two if their first child is a girl. Minority nationalities with small populations can also have two children.

40

LeShan Da Fo, the giant mountain Buddha, in Sichuan Province

Religions

Buddhism is the most widespread religion in China, but China is a multi-religious country. Other religions are Taoism, Islam, and Christianity. During the Cultural Revolution (1966-1976), religion was taboo in China and churches were closed. Since 1979 when China started to open to the outside world, Chinese people have enjoyed more freedom to choose their religions. Christian churches can be seen in many places, and more and more people go to church today. Religious holidays are respected. For example, at *Shantou* University, *Guangdong* Province, foreign teachers get a holiday on December 25, Christmas Day. Some foreign teachers use this occasion to invite their Chinese students to have a Christmas party, giving them an opportunity to practice English and learn about a different culture.

In China religious practices are allowed within the scope of law. The Hui, Uygur, Kazak, Kirgiz, Tatar, Dongxiang, Salar, and Bonan ethnic groups practice Islam; the Tibetan, Mongolian, Dai, and Yugur ethnic groups practice Buddhism and Lamaism; the Miao, Yao and Yi practice Christianity; Shamanism is followed by the Oroqen, Ewenki and Daur nationalities; and the majority Han people believe in Buddhism, Christianity, and Taoism.

41

Chinese holidays

In China official and traditional holidays are observed. Most traditional Chinese holidays revolve around the Lunar Calendar. In general, traditional holidays are given more attention than official holidays, and the traditions and values of the traditional festivals are deeply rooted in the hearts and minds of the Chinese people. Almost all traditional festivals are characterized by good wishes for happiness, wealth, and health. The Chinese get together to enjoy family reunions and relaxation during these festivals. Today, as the living standard improves and people's thinking changes as a result of opening to the outside world, there has been an increasing number of people who earn a decent salary. The result is that more people are traveling across China and abroad for traditional or official holidays instead of staying home as they used to in the past.

Since 1999, China has implemented three week-long breaks every year, extending the length of holidays: one week for the Chinese Lunar New Year or the Spring Festival, one week for the May 1st International Labor Day, and one week for the October 1st National Day. These three weeks, called "Golden Weeks," are designed to encourage people to spend more money to help the tourism economy grow.

Chinese official holidays

New Year's Day (January 1)
People get one day off. It is a regular holiday, not as much observed as the upcoming Chinese Lunar New Year that is usually around a month away.

International Women's Day (March 8)
Working women, including teachers and other professionals, get a whole or a half day off with pay. Many employers give souvenirs or an additional bonus to women to acknowledge their positive contributions to their organizations.

International Labor Day (May 1)

It is a one-week holiday today. It is one of the three "Golden Weeks" holidays, giving Chinese people more time to enjoy life and spend money.

International Children's Day (June 1)

It is the most important holiday for Chinese children all over the country. They get presents from parents and schools, where big celebration parties are held.

The Chinese Communist Party's Birthday (July 1)

It marks the founding of the Chinese Communist Party (CCP) in 1921 in Shanghai. It is usually characterized by front-page editorials from major government newspapers. The Chinese do not get a day off on this day.

Army's Day (August 1)

It is the anniversary of the first uprising in 1927 by a communist-led army against the Nationalists.

Teachers' Day (September 1)

Established in 1939, originally Teachers' Day was set on August 27, Confucius' birthday. It was canceled during The Great Proletarian Cultural Revolution (1966-1976). It was restored in the early eighties as an effort to improve teachers' social status and to call on the whole nation to respect teachers and knowledge. Now more and more people are trying to revert Teachers' Day to Confucius' birthday. Teachers usually get presents from their schools, but they still have to work on this day.

National Day (October 1)

One of the Golden Week vacations in China, it is the anniversary of the founding of the People's Republic of China in 1949 following the defeat of the Nationalists. There used to be grand parades in the major cities. Now celebrations usually take the form of parties in public parks by day and fireworks

43

and grand TV galas in the evening. The central government holds a big banquet in the Great Hall of the People with front-page editorials celebrating achievements made during the year and since the founding of New China.

Chinese traditional holidays

The Lantern Festival
(15th day of the first month on the Lunar Calendar)

It is the day for displaying all kinds of lanterns and eating *Tang Yuan* (ball-shaped boiled sweet rice dumplings with delicious stuffing), symbolizing family unity. The Lantern Festival also marks the end of the Chinese Lunar Year. People do not get a day off on this day.

Qing Ming (Tomb Sweeping Day) Festival

It falls on April 4 or 5. Originally it was a celebration of the spring season. Later it became a day for paying respect to ancestors and the dead. Many people go and sweep the tombs of their ancestors. People do not get a day off on this day.

Duan Wu (Dragon Boat) Festival
(5th Day of the 5th month on the Lunar Calendar)

It falls on the 5th of day of May of the Lunar Calendar. There are many tales about the origins of the holiday. The story that most Chinese believe is about *Qu Yuan*, a great patriot poet of the State of *Chu* during the Warring States period (475-221 B.C.E.). *Qu Yuan* killed himself to protest his emperor who gave in to the bully State of *Chin*. Legend goes that after the poet committed suicide, people of *Chu* were afraid that fish might eat his body. They launched their boats and started throwing rice dumplings wrapped in bamboo leaves into the river to feed the fish. Now, every May 5th, Chinese people make and eat bamboo-leaf-wrapped rice dumplings and hold dragon boat competitions on this day to remember the poet. People do not get a day off on this day.

44

Moon cakes eaten during the mid-autumn Moon Festival

Mid-Autumn Festival or the Moon Festival
(15th day of the 8th month of the Lunar Calendar)

It is the second most important traditional holiday after the Chinese New Year. The 15th day of the 8th month of the Lunar Calendar marks the middle of autumn. Traditionally, after the peasants get in their crops, it is time to enjoy life. The moon on this day is the fullest and largest to the eye. It is a time for family reunions, and people eat moon cakes while enjoying watching the full moon. The round shape to a Chinese signifies family reunions. For those who cannot get together on this day, it is a time to remember loved ones and home towns. People do not get a day off on this day.

Symbols of happiness and good luck are traditions of the Spring Festival.
Large masks for the lion and dragon street dances and bright, red paper lanterns

45

Spring Festival (The Chinese New Year)
(1ˢᵗ day of the 1ˢᵗ month of the Lunar Calendar)

The oldest and most important traditional festival in China is the Spring Festival. It is also celebrated in parts of East and Southeast Asia. The Chinese New Year starts with the New Moon on the first day of the New Year. The festival ends on the full moon 15 days later. The date of the Chinese New Year is determined by the Lunar Calendar. New Year's Eve and New Year's Day are celebrated as a family affair, a time of reunion. People dress up, exchange food and gifts, visit family members, and remember ancestors. It is as important as Christmas in western countries, and it is also one of the Golden-Week holidays. Each year is symbolized by one of twelve different animals. A new cycle begins in 2008 with the first year of a twelve-year cycle.

A lunar calendar showing the 12 signs of the Chinese "Zodiac" surrounding the Taoist Yin-Yang symbol

Year	*Animal*
2008	Rat
2009	Ox
2010	Tiger
2011	Rabbit
2112	Dragon
2113	Snake
2114	Horse
2115	Sheep
2116	Monkey
2117	Rooster
2118	Dog
2119	Boar

3.3 Administrative Divisions and Major Cities

China has 23 provinces, 5 autonomous regions, 4 centrally administrative municipalities, and 2 special administrative regions. Municipalities are directly under the administration of the central government. A municipality has the same political, economical, and jurisdictional rights as a province. A list of the provinces, regions, municipalities, and major cities will be found in Appendix B.

3.4 Government

To a foreigner it may not be easy to understand China's system of government and why it has been working the way it is in a country with the world's largest population for such a long time. The best way to gain a better understanding is to see how its people live, work, and play. The following is just a framework of China's political system and government.

CPC and NPC

The Communist Party of China (CPC) is the country's sole political party in power. The CPC has both central and local organizations. The state power is exercised through the National People's Congress (NPC) and local People's Congresses at all levels.

The President of the People's Republic of China, elected by the National People's Congress, is the head of state. The President serves for a term of five years and can serve no more than two consecutive terms.

The central administrative system in China includes the central administrative units under the National People's Congress and the leadership of the central administrative units that control local administrative organs at various levels.

The State Council is the highest administrative organ of the state. The State Council exercises unified leadership over local state administrative organs at provincial, autonomous regional, and municipal levels.

*Four levels of administrative divisions
under the central government:*

- Provinces, autonomous regions, and municipalities directly under the Central Government

- Cities with districts and autonomous prefectures

- Counties, autonomous counties, and cities

- Townships, ethnic townships, and towns.

There are 23 provinces, four municipalities directly under the Central Government, and five autonomous regions (see the complete list in the appendix). The governors and other local officials of the above four levels are elected by relevant People's Congresses at various levels.

*The System of Multi-Party Cooperation and
Political Consultation and CPPCC*

The system means that the CPC is the only party in power in the People's Republic of China. Under the leadership of the CPC, the eight other political parties participate in the discussion and management of state affairs, in cooperation with the CPC. The eight political parties are China Revolutionary Committee of the Kuomintang, China Democratic League, China Democratic National Construction Association, China Association for the Promotion of Democracy, Chinese Peasants' and Workers' Democratic Party, China *Zhi Gong Dang, Jiusan* Society, and Taiwan Democratic Self-government League. All the non-communist political parties have their members holding leading positions in the government and judicial units at various levels upon recommendation by the CPC.

The Chinese People's Political Consultative Conference (CPPCC) is an important organ of multi-party cooperation and political consultation under the leadership of the CPC. CPPCC has a national committee and regional committees.

Special administrative regions

Now China has two Special Administrative Regions: *Hong Kong* and *Macao*. The chief executives of Special Administrative Regions are elected or selected through consultation locally and appointed by the Central Government. Special Administrative Regions do not exercise the rights of state sovereignty. Foreign affairs in Special Administrative Regions are administered by the Central Government. Defense affairs in the regions fall under the responsibility of the Central Government.

3.5 Educational System

Valuing education and respecting teachers has been China's tradition for thousands of years. Providing education to a huge population in China has been a daunting task since ancient times. As early as over two thousand years ago, in the Confucius period (551-479 B.C.E.), the most well-known ancient philosopher opened his private school in the Kingdom of *Lu* (today's *Shandong* Province) and accepted 3,000 students. He only charged them 10 strips of jerked meat per person as tuition. Since the founding of New China in 1949, China has launched its nine-year compulsory education, and the illiteracy rate among the young and middle-aged has dropped dramatically from 80% to 5%.

Four Levels of basic education

With over 200 million elementary and high school students, China boasts a high-quality basic education system, comparing favorably with the rest of the world. Basic education in China can be divided into four levels: pre-school, elementary, junior high school and senior high school.

Children attend kindergarten from three until six years of age. Classes are normally divided into Small (three-year-olds), Middle (four-year-olds), and Large (five-year-olds), where children learn basic arithmetic, Chinese characters, drawing, and games.

Elementary education starts at age six and lasts six years. Children learn math, Chinese, fine arts, physical education, and other courses. Since China's reform and opening policy was implemented in 1979, more and more primary schools have begun English instruction, especially in urban areas.

Elementary school children doing morning exercises

Students start their three-year junior high school at age 12. They continue to build on the solid foundation of basic knowledge acquired in primary schools. The nine-year compulsory education includes the six-year elementary and three-year junior high school education. The government provides free tuition for these nine years. Upon completion of junior high school, students take a locally-administered entrance examination. Based on this examination they have the option of either continuing in the senior high school or entering a vocational secondary school. Vocational schools offer two-year or four-year programs to train skilled workers, farmers, and managerial and technical personnel.

Special education

China has made a series of laws and regulations to ensure the right of disabled people to education. Now China has 1,540 schools for special education with 375,000 students. Children with disabilities who can adapt to a regular learning environment may enroll at regular schools at various levels.

Two new universities in Shanghai, Fudan and Tongji

Higher education

Upon graduation from senior high school, students take a competitive national college-entrance examination. In 2007 over ten million high school graduates took the national exam, and more than half of them were admitted. For comparison, in 1977 after the Cultural Revolution fewer than six million took the exam and the enrollment rate was only about 4%. Higher education in China includes two- or three-year junior college programs and four-year programs. Now many institutions of higher learning also offer M.A., M.B.A., and Ph.D. programs. Currently, China has over 2,000 colleges and universities with over 20 million students. The latest buzz on university campuses includes the merger of colleges and universities designed to maximize resources. For example, in Shanghai, the Shanghai Medical Sciences University has been merged into the new Fudan University, and the Shanghai Railway University into the new Tongji University.

A traditional garden at Fudan University and multicultural university students

Changes

Since China opened its doors to the outside, its educational system has undergone enormous changes.

- In the past, schools in China were run only by the government. Now China has allowed private schools, including those run jointly with foreign partners. Today, there are over 70,000 private schools at various levels across the country, including over 1,279 private institutions of higher learning. The total enrollment of private schools has reached over 14 million.

- Under the centralized planned economic system, China used to guarantee jobs for its college and university graduates after graduation, and graduates had to accept jobs assigned by the government. Now graduates have to work very hard to compete for jobs of their choice through interviews.

- Higher education is no longer free, but to ensure that students with financial difficulties can enter colleges and universities, the government has provided assistance in various forms ranging from work-study programs and tuition reduction to scholarships and stipends.

- China used to allocate fixed funding to schools that were not supposed to receive income from other channels. Now schools can still get funds from the government but are allowed to make their own money to benefit teachers and staff. In the past, teachers were poorly paid. Today, it is not true! But in remote rural areas, teachers' salaries are still unsatisfactory.

- Schools in China have increased their cooperation with foreign schools through faculty and student exchange programs and are jointly running academic programs. Students find it easier to apply to study in foreign countries. The number of foreign students from 178 countries studying on campus in China has surpassed 110,000. Since China opened its doors to the outside in 1979, over 697,000 Chinese have studied in 103 countries; 185,000 of them have returned to China after finishing their studies abroad.

- With the spread of broadband technology and internet accessibility, online education in various forms is developing so fast in China that the total enrollment is now over 1.3 million. When China first initiated its reform and opening policy, the Central Radio and TV University was the only institution offering remote courses. Now 68 institutions of higher learning have been authorized to provide distance education. Across the country, over 2,000 off-campus learning centers, offering 140 majors, have been established.

3.6 Economy

When you go shopping at Wal-Mart or other shopping centers in the US, certainly you have seen many products that bear the label MADE IN CHINA. They range from household articles to electronic goods. However, this was not the case thirty years ago. This clearly shows that China's economy has been developing very rapidly. In 2004, China contributed one-third of the total *global* economic growth. In 2005, China achieved 14 percent of the world economy in terms of purchasing power, second only to the U.S. According to the latest information from the World Bank, in the first three quarters of 2007, China's GDP growth rate was 11.5 percent, higher than expected.

About 20 percent of China's exports go to the U.S. It is estimated that by 2010, China's trade volume to the U.S. alone will reach $2.3 trillion in goods and $400 billion in services. China has become a vital supplier to American manufacturers and consumers. U.S. trade with China is second only to trade with Canada and Mexico.

In the wake of its fast economic development, China is facing serious challenges in environmental protection. China is now taking steps to solve this serious problem. On October 15, 2007, Hu Jintao, General Secretary of the Central Committee of the Communist Party of China, said, in the Report to the Seventeenth National Congress of CPC: "Our economic growth is realized at an excessively high cost of resources and the environment." He went on to point out other problems facing the nation in its rapid development: "There remains an imbalance in development between urban and rural areas, among regions, and between the economy and society. It has become more difficult to bring about a steady growth of agriculture and continued increase in farmers' incomes. There are still many problems affecting people's immediate interests in areas such as employment, social security, income distribution, education, public health, housing, work safety, administration of justice, and public order; and some low-income people lead a rather difficult life."

How has China achieved such rapid economic development?

From planned to market economy. After the founding of New China in 1949, China's economy followed a rigid Soviet pattern characterized by strict central planning. The central government set out goals as to what and how much to produce for the whole country, and every province received production quotas from the central government. Then the city, district, and county government got their quotas from superiors. Under such a system, there was little or no flexibility or initiative on the part of the grass-root-level factories, resulting in a sparse supply of goods and a low level of living standards. Ration coupons were issued to citizens who could get only limited quantities of goods such as soap, rice, flour, vegetable oil, pork, cotton, bicycles, and sewing machines, to name only a few.

Starting at the end of 1978, initiated by the late leader, *Deng Xiaoping,* called the architect of China's opening and reforms, China started to open its doors to the outside world and undergo economic reforms, gradually turning its planned economy into a market economy regulated by the force of the market. Since then more and more foreign companies have set up their businesses across the country. As a result, people's living standards have greatly improved and the Chinese people have said goodbye to the old ration coupons.

3.7 Chinese History

With a recorded history of nearly 4,000 years, it is difficult to get a comprehensive picture of China's past in a short time. This brief outline of key events may help.

1. The first emperor of the first unified China, Qin Shi Huang, was responsible for three major developments:

   • **Unification.** He unified China for the first time into one country with a unified language and currency.

   • **The Great Wall.** He ordered that the previous walls built by various warring states be connected and fortified into the Great Wall for defense purposes. It was extended and strengthened by subsequent dynasties. It is over 4,000 miles long.

- **The Terra Cotta Horses and Warriors**. About 700,000 people participated in the construction of the silent life-like underground army to protect him in his tomb after his death. More than 2,000 years after his death, it was discovered accidentally in 1974 by some villagers who were digging a well for drinking water in *Xi'An*, one of the ancient capitals of China. It is listed as the Eighth Wonder of the World.

2. Ancient China produced four **inventions** that have contributed to the civilization of the world: paper-making, printing, the compass, and gunpowder.

3. The most glorious period in ancient China was the **Tang Dynasty**. Politics, economy, music, and art developed to the highest level, attracting world attention. The Chinese people used to be called *Tang Ren* (*Ren* means person) in the West. Even today, Chinatown is translated in Chinese as *Tang Ren Jie* (street).

4. Following the **Opium War** launched by the British in 1840, the corrupt Chinese government was forced to sign a series of unfair treaties, allowing foreign powers to seize Chinese territory. China's Hong Kong and Macao were taken by the British and Portuguese, respectively. China's territorial integrity was repeatedly violated, and it started to lag behind. China was gradually turned into a semi-feudal and semi-colonial country, lagging behind the western world.

5. A revolution led by Dr. Sun Yat-sen overthrew China's last imperial dynasty, the *Qing* Dynasty, in 1911 and founded **the Republic of China**, ending the feudal and monarchic rule of more than 2,000 years.

6. **New China,** led by Mao Zedong, was founded in 1949 after the Anti-Japanese Occupation War and the civil war with *Guomingdang* led by *Jiang Jieshi* (Chiang Kai-shek), who fled to Taiwan following the victory of the communists. Since the founding of New China, mainland China has been ruled by those who led the communist party.

7. The **Great Leap Forward Movement** (1958-1960) was a utopian commune campaign. However, natural disasters caused many people to die.

Dr. Sun Yat-sen (1866-1925)

Mao Zedong (1893-1976)

Deng Xiao Ping (1904-1997)

8. The **Cultural Revolution** from 1966 to 1976, started by Mao Zedong, was aimed at eradicating the Old Ideas, Old Culture, Old Customs, and Old Habits. Many intellectuals and artists were persecuted and their families destroyed. It was a radical campaign causing a great loss to the country's economy, culture, and education.

9. Since 1978, the **Reform and Opening to the Outside World** was led by Deng Xiao Ping, the chief architect of China's reform policies. China has embarked on a transformation from the old centralized planned economy to a new market economy. The Chinese people's living standard has greatly improved. Their economy has become one of the fastest growing in the world. As one of the five permanent U.N. Security Council Members, China has been playing a very active and positive role in the international political arena, promoting world peace and development in cooperation with other nations.

For a more detailed timeline of the dynasties, kingdoms, and republic, see Appendix C.

4. Doing Business in China

4.1 Establishing Business Relations

Since China started to open to the outside world in 1978, much has been changed in the way business is done, especially with foreigners. In the past, you had to get a letter of introduction from a friend, a relative, or an acquaintance in order to get into the Chinese market. You had to attend a big export commodity expo to get more partners. Today, these practices may still work, but many other channels are open to foreigners wishing to do business in China. For example, you can simply start your internet search to locate potential business partners, followed by emails, faxes, letters, or phone calls. Later, a personal visit would be the final gesture to show sincerity.

Pay a visit to the commercial office of the Chinese embassy or consulate to get basic information. They can offer you reliable channels of communication or help you establish business relations with a potential business.

4.2 Business Negotiation

In a business negotiation, the final decision will be made by the number one official in the company, a president or general manager. So, if you want to have a face-to-face negotiation to strike a deal, make sure that this official will be present. Otherwise, other people at the meeting will only say something like: "We'll take it home and report to my boss and he will make the final decision." When this happens, it is a waste of time and money for you and the other side. Therefore, don't invite a delegation to visit you in the U.S. if their number one official does not come. Also, do not visit a company or engage in negotiations in China if the number one official will not be present.

It is customary to have a dinner together following the completion of the negotiation or a business conference in China. If the other side gives a dinner first, invite them to dinner after the next meeting. Reciprocity of kindness is deeply rooted in Chinese culture.

This billboard is a sign of the times. It advertises China's People's Insurance Company and its Life and Property Insurance. The two lines of big characters say, "To have the Life and Property Insurance. To be happy to watch Beijing Olympic Games." The five small dolls around the two lines of characters are the Official Five 2008 Beijing Olympic Games Mascots. The top line of smaller characters says, "Lucky Draw for 10,000 Olympic Games Admission Tickets" (meaning 10,000 tickets will be given to those lucky buyers of the insurance). Farthest left, you can also see the five Olympic Rings. Today there are many billboards across the country for all kinds of businesses, but this one is very special. It combines business with the Olympic Games.

This Beijing department store is not special except for the two big ads on the front of the building. Before China opened its economy to the rest of the world in 1978, this was the largest department store in Beijing. Now there are many, many shopping places that are larger. But this store still keeps its original name, while trying to make the old building look new. Perhaps because of this, it is a landmark of old Beijing, and people still walk past.

4.3 Eye Contact and Body Language

At the negotiation table with your business partners, look into their eyes when they talk to show your sincerity. Have a notebook in front of you to take some notes. This will present a very positive image to the Chinese side, as it is considered standard manners at meetings at various levels in China. During the negotiation, do not take a nod from your potential business partner as an agreement. It more often means they are listening to you carefully.

4.4 Business Social Customs

Give your business partners some photo opportunities. Most business people and officials like it very much, because the pictures will help them promote their business and image.

In many places in China, business people like to drink a lot of alcohol, and they would like their business partners to do the same at the dinner table. If you cannot drink alcohol, tell them so, and you can be served with cold drinks or water instead of alcohol. When they propose toasts to you, if you do not have anything in your cup to drink, you will be considered impolite. Also, you should be prepared for a lot of smokers in Chinese restaurants, even in very good ones. More often than not, the food is excellent but not the smoke.

When presenting a gift to your business partners, use red or gold colored paper to wrap your gifts or souvenirs. Red represents happiness and good luck. Gold or yellow represents power in Chinese culture. Do not use black and white, colors that are normally associated with death.

Remember the following tips:

- Don't give expensive gifts that could be regarded as bribery. But souvenirs are OK.

- Present your souvenir at the end of your first meeting with your potential business partners. If the other side presents their souvenir at the beginning of the meeting, just follow suit.

5. Applying for a Job in China

Since China opened its doors to the outside world, more and more foreigners have come to travel and work in this fast-changing country with immense opportunities. To go to China to work is a rewarding experience and in many cases you will gain more than you expected. However, in such a large country undergoing fast, sometimes unpredictable changes, it is quite a challenge to find a job and work for a period of time in China. It requires careful preparation and determination to adjust to the new physical, cultural, and emotional environment.

5.1 Getting Ready to Apply

It was easy for a native English speaker to find a job when China first opened its doors to the outside. But today, things have changed a lot. You will have to go through a more challenging application process, including interviews, in order to get a good job with a nice salary. Get your resume and credentials ready, including degrees and previous employment history. As China is employing more of its own people with good English (those who studied and worked abroad) and foreigners with advanced degrees and expertise, verification of your credentials and sometimes a serious check on your resume is not unusual. So don't think that you can fool the Chinese easily with false credentials or resume.

5.2 Deciding Where to Work in China

Study a map of China and ask yourself the following questions: Should I go to the north, south, east, or west part of China to live and work? It is extremely cold in northern China in winter and very hot in southern China, especially along the coastal areas. Some foreigners cannot bear the extremely cold or hot climate, while others want to challenge themselves by experiencing a very different physical condition. In China, the eastern part close to the coast is more populated and developed. Western China is relatively underdeveloped. Nowadays the Chinese government is encouraging domestic and foreign enterprises to invest in western China, especially in developing infrastructure and education. The coastal regions that were the first to open to the world thirty years ago have become very developed. But you, as a native English speaker with expertise, will still be welcome almost everywhere if you find the right employer.

5.3 Deciding What You Want to Do in China

This can be a very difficult decision to make. An American professor of biology or economics can end up teaching very basic English conversation at a college that offers a teaching position in the Biology or Economics Department. Of course, you may teach your real subject in an M.A. or Ph.D. program in more prestigious institutions of higher learning. But it is often the case that you will spend a lot more time teaching your students how to pronounce difficult words and how to communicate in English. Foreigners with a liberal arts background and teaching experience are particularly welcome by the English and other departments of a college or university. Those with an M.B.A. and management experience are more welcome to work in companies and enterprises jointly run by Chinese and foreigners. No matter what you have already decided to do in China, be prepared to make an adjustment, because the concept of job assignment in China is very different from what you have in the U.S., where you just sign a contract and start doing what is specified in the contract.

5.4 How to Apply for a Position

Get on the internet to find possible places to work in China. Start to contact the Chinese side in writing or through email first. Generally speaking, you can get a response quickly if you see that they want to employ native English speakers. You can get useful information from the following sites:

Chinese Embassy in Washington, D.C.
http://www.china-embassy.org

Consulate General of the P. R. China in New York
http://www.nyconsulate.prchina.org/eng/index.html

Consulate General of the P.R. China in Los Angeles
http://www.chinaconsulatela.org

Consulate General of the P.R. China in San Francisco
http://consulatesf.webchina.org

Consulate General of the P.R. China in Houston
http://www.chinahouston.org

The Economic and Commercial Section of the Embassy of
the People's Republic of China to the United States
http://mofcom.gov.cn

Chinese Embassy in Canada
http://www.chinaembassycanada.org

The following site is useful for those interested in an ESL
teaching job in China.

http://www.eslcafe.com/jobs/china

5.5 Tips for Those Going to Teach in China

Teaching in China can be a very rewarding experience.
Through teaching, you come into contact with students from
different social and economic backgrounds. However, to teach in
China can also be very challenging, because of the different educational system and the potential for culture shock.

- The Chinese educational system has been very exam-oriented,
  and that motivates teachers and students to work for high exam
  scores. In addition, they are used to sitting there and listening to the teacher. As a result you may find students inactive
  in class. It takes a lot of effort to make them feel comfortable
  sharing ideas openly in class, but their minds are very active
  and once they start to open their mouths to talk, you will find
  them to be great students.

- To get to know your students, during western traditional festivals such as Thanksgiving and Christmas, organize a small class party to let your students see your culture. That may interest them more than anything else. During their Chinese traditional festivals, have them do something. By doing things together, they feel less shy and more willing to contribute in class.

- At some schools, when your Chinese students or other friends come to visit you, they are required to sign in at the gate of the hostel or apartment building for foreign teachers. Don't be surprised. It is actually good for your safety.

- Remember that your Chinese students love to see your family photos. Your students may ask questions you do not normally ask in the U. S., such as "How old are you? How much do you earn?" In their culture, it is not inappropriate to ask such questions.

5.6 Additional Tips

- Medicine that is taken on a regular basis should be purchased prior to leaving for short stays. If you are going for an extended stay, make sure you can order more from your supplier. It usually takes 10-15 days to reach you.

- There is a variety of climates; therefore pack for the season(s) when you intend to be there. If you are going to teach there for a year contract, then it would not be necessary to over-pack, as you can purchase almost anything you need – unless you are very tall or broad.

- The Chinese people are open, warm, and friendly to people of other countries. Nevertheless, your experience in China will be most rewarding if you respect the customs of their society and the laws of the government. And it is best to avoid political arguments and debates. There is nothing to be gained from it.

- If you are teaching at a university you will find the students to be open-minded and very willing to be of assistance. Expect to make lifelong and sincere friends.

5.7 Job Offer and Contract

After the Chinese side agrees to employ you, you will receive a job offer with general terms of employment. But this is by no means a contract; that will be signed after you arrive in China. After you arrive, you will talk face to face with your Chinese employer, who will show you the actual contract with a detailed job description. You need to read your contract very carefully, especially about your benefits such as pay, holidays, medical insurance, and air tickets.

5.8 Getting the Right Visa to Enter China

To gain a valuable experience working in China, you need to know the rules and regulations that help you settle down and enjoy your life and work in an entirely new environment. The first thing you do after landing a job is to apply for the right visa to enter China. Depending on the purposes of the trip, there are eight types of ordinary visas issued by China.

- *Visa Z:* for those who work in China for over six months, and their family members accompanying them.

- *Visa F:* for those who visit or work in China for less than six months.

- *Visa X:* for those who study or do an internship in China for less than six months.

- *Visa D:* for permanent residence.

- *Visa L:* for those who travel to visit relatives and friends in China or who go to China for private matters. A group of more than nine people going together can obtain a **group visa.**

- *Visa G:* for a stopover in China.

- *Visa J-1:* for foreign journalists residing in China.

- *Visa J-2:* for those who come to cover news temporarily in China.

- *Visa C:* for foreign crew members (airplanes, ships, and trains) and accompanying family members who come to China regularly.

5.9. Obtaining a Visa
to Enter China's Special Administrative Regions

A panaramic view of Hong Kong

Hong Kong. A U.S. citizen who possesses a valid U.S. passport going to Hong Kong for business or tourism may stay in Hong Kong for three months without a visa. If they plan to stay in Hong Kong for over three months or if their purposes are for employment, study, training, residence, or visiting relatives, they must apply for a visa.

If you are going to Hong Kong for one night and back to mainland China, you must have a double-entry visa. That means you can enter mainland China twice within 90 days. Although part of China, Hong Kong is a Special Administrative Region.

Macau. Valid passports are required. Passports should be valid for 30 days beyond the intended period of stay in Macau. Because many neighboring areas require six months validity remaining on the passport, U.S. citizens planning travel beyond Macau should ensure that their passports are valid for at least six months from the date of their proposed entry into such areas. A visa is not required for tourist visits of up to 30 days. Visit the Embassy of the People's Republic of China web site at http://www.china-embassy.org/eng/ for the most current visa information. Please check the Macau SAR government home page at http://www.gov.mo/ for up-to-date entry and exit requirements.

6. Chinese Language

6.1 Mandarin Chinese

Putonghua (Mandarin Chinese) is the language of the Han people, but most of the other ethnic groups also have their own languages or dialects. That can make communication difficult when they speak to each other without using the common language, *Putonghua*. However, people from different regions can understand the same written characters.

Mandarin Chinese is the most commonly used language. It is taught in all schools and it is the medium of the government. And today people across China are encouraged to use *Putonghua* in offices and public places.

Spoken Chinese is a tonal language, with four tones in addition to individual sounds. For instance, the word *"Ma"* can mean "mother," "scold," "horse," or "bother," depending on how it is said. To assist the learning of Chinese, a Romanization system called Pinyin has replaced other earlier Romanized spellings (the capital of China is spelled *Beijing* instead of the earlier spelling of "Peking."). It was devised in 1958 and has since been adopted as a standard form to represent Chinese sounds.

The Chinese writing system is pictographic. This means that a "picture" represents an idea or word. Therefore, the Chinese writing system is different from that of most western languages. The words for these languages are represented by letters, while Chinese words are represented by characters. Some Chinese characters were developed as simple pictures from nature, such as animals, birds, mountains, and rivers. Although the style of writing has changed and gradually been transformed over at least 5,000 years into the characters used today, Chinese is the only major writing system of the world that has continued its pictograph-based system without interruption and still uses it. Many students of Chinese are first attracted to the language because of the writing system, which is surely one of the most fascinating scripts in the world.

6.2 Sample Pictographic Chinese Characters

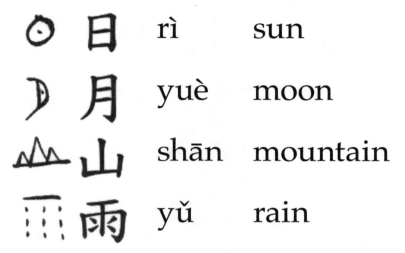

☉	日	rì	sun
☽	月	yuè	moon
⩕	山	shān	mountain
⫶⫶	雨	yǔ	rain

6.3 Survival Chinese

The Pinyin transcriptions in this section are marked for tone. As you can see, a single "word" such as *ma* can have more than one meaning, depending on the tone of the word. It would be a good idea to have a speaker of Chinese help you get started on producing the tones below.

Word with tone	Description with tone	Description of tone	Name of tone
mā	mother	a flat and unchanging high tone	1st tone
má	bother	a rising tone	2nd tone
mǎ	horse	a falling and then rising tone	3rd tone
mà	to scold	a falling tone	4th tone
ma	grammatical marker used in a question	no emphasis	Neutral

Adapted from **www.instantspeakChinese.com/pinyin/pinyinTones.cfm**

Daily Essentials:

Hello	Nǐ hǎo	你好
Thank you	Xièxie	谢谢
You are welcome	Bú yòng xiè	不用谢
	Bù kèqi	不客气

(Kèqì means 'polite.'
Bù kèqì, literally 'do not be polite,' is the response to xièxie, 'thank you.')

Take care	Nín zǒu hao	您走好

(leave-taking)

Do keep in touch	Jīng cháng liánxì a!	经常联系啊!

(leave-taking)

Goodbye	Zài jiàn	再见
Excuse me	Qǐng wèn	请问。。。

(Literally it means 'please ask,' but really it's a polite way of asking a question. It's equivalent to 'Excuse me' or 'May I ask ... ?')

Where is the restroom?

	Cè suǒ zai nǎr?	厕所在哪儿?
	Wèi shēng jian zai nǎr?	卫生间在哪儿?
	Xǐ shǒu jian zai nǎr?	洗手间在哪儿?

I am sorry	Duì bùqǐ	对不起
It is okay	Méi guān xi	没关系
Please	Qǐng	请
Mr.	Xiānsheng	先生
Ms.	Xiao jiě	小姐

Good morning	Zaoshang hao	早上好
Good afternoon	Xiawŭ hao	下午好
Good evening	Wansháng hao	晚上好
Good night	Wan ān	晚安

At the Restaurant:

| Menu, please | Qǐng kan cai dan | 请看菜单 |

What would you like to eat?

| | Nǐmen chī dian'r shénme ? | 你们吃点什么? |

Please bring ...	Qǐng lai dian	请来点。。。
I want ...	Wǒ yao	我要。。。
the bill please	Maidān	买单
Here you are	Gěi nín	给您
Rice	mǐfàn	米饭
noodles	miàntiáo	面条
greens/vegetables	qīngcài	青菜
roast duck	kao ya	烤鸭
chopsticks	kuàizi	筷子

What would you like to drink?

| | Nǐmen hē dian'r shénme? | 你们喝点儿什么? |

A restaurant in Guangzhou

I would like green tea

Wǒ yàa lǜ chá   我要绿茶

I would like jasmine tea

Wǒ yao huā chá   我要花茶

(Literally, huā chá means 'flower tea.' Because jasmine tea is the most famous flower-scented tea, many people use the term huā chá to refer to jasmine tea.)

fruit juice	guǒ zhī	果汁
beer	píjiǔ	啤酒
wine	pútaojiǔ	葡萄酒
coffee	kāfēi	咖啡

Transportation:

ticket	piào	票
two tickets	liang zhang piao	两张票

(Zhāng is a word for measurements that applies to paper and tickets. It is used together with a number, e.g. yī zhāng piào, one ticket, liang zhang piao, two tickets.)

hard seat	yìng zuò	硬座
soft seat	ruan zuò	软座
bus/coach/vehicle	chē	车
public bus	gōnggòng qìchē	公共汽车
taxi	chūzūchē	出租车
subway	dìtiě	地铁
bicycle	zìxíngchē	自行车
train	huǒchē	火车
train station	huǒchē zhan	火车站
hotel	fàndiàn	饭店

Do you have a room available?

	Yǒu fangjian ma?	有房间吗?
I have a reservation	Wǒ dìng le fangjian	我订了房间
single room	dānrén fángjiān	单人房
double room	shuāngrén fángjiān	双人房
shower	línyù	淋浴

7. Other Resources

Websites

Adoption: www.china-ccaa.org/frmes/index_unlogin_en.jsp

Education: www.sino-education.org/english/index.htm

Embassy – Chinese: www.china-embassy.org/eng/

Embassy – USA in China: Beijing.usembassy-china.org.en/

Embassy – USA in Washinton, D.C.: usembassy.state.gov/

General information on China: en.wikipedia.org/wiki/China

History: www.chinahistoryforum.com

Import and Export Fair: www.cantonfair.org.cn/en/

Language: www.chineselearner.com/

Language: www.learn-chinese-online.net

Language Instruction: Beijing Language and Culture University
www.eblcu.net/newenglish/index.html

Marriage Registration:
Houston.china-consulate.org/visa/English/marriage/jh.htm

Ministry of Foreign Affairs: www.frmprc.gov.cn/eng/default.htm

News – quick reference sites, Chinese government links, online newspapers, magazines, and broadcasting: chinanews.bfn.org

News – Chinese Government official newspaper, *People's Daily* online in English with comprehensive information: China at a glance, Chinese history, Constitution, Laws & Regulations, CPC & State Organs, Ethnic Minorities, Selected Works of Deng Xiaoping: English.peopledaily.com.cn/

Olympic Games: en.beijing2008.cn/

Pinyin: www.pinyin.org

Pinyin Tones:
www.instantspeakChinese.com/pinyin/pinyinTones.cfm

Visas: www.visarite.com/chn/Consulate.htm

Books

Chun, Wang, and Chongqing, Zheng. *Chinese Characters in Pictures*, Sinolingua, Beijing, 2005.

Concise English-Chinese Chinese-English Dictionary, The Commercial Press/Oxford University Press, 2004.

Fuxing, Wang. *Chinese Language Learning for Foreigners*. Sinolingua, Beijing, 1994.

Green, Marshall, Holdridge, John H. and Stokes, William N. *War and Peace with China*, DACOR Press, 1994.

Hessler, Peter. *River Town: Two Years on the Yangtze*. Harper Collins 2001.

Hong, Wei. *Practical Business Chinese*. China Book, 2000.

Huafu, Jiao. *Chinese Common Knowledge Series*, Hong Kong China Tourism Press, 2005.

Pei, Zhang, and Wenyuan, Deng. *Cross-Cultural Awareness*. Qinghua University Press, 2003.

Wang, Lin. *Practical Business English* (with Chinese Translation). Shantou University Press, 1997.

Wenzhong, Hu, and Grove, Cornelius, *Encountering the Chinese— a Guide for Americans*. Intercultural Press, Inc. 1999.

Xinhua Dictionary with English Translation. Commercial Press, 2000.

Yanchang, Deng, and Runqing, Liu. *Language and Culture*. Foreign Language Teaching and Research Press, 1989.

Appendix A

Addresses of U.S. and Canadian Embassies and Consulates

U.S. Embassy in China

3 Xiu Shui Bei Jie
Beijing 100600, China
Tel: (86-10) 6532-3831
After hours/Emergencies: (86-10) 6532-1910
Fax: (86-10) 6532-4153, 6532-3178
The Embassy consular district includes the following provinces/
regions of China: Beijing, Tianjin, Shandong, Shanxi, Inner Mongolia, Ningxia, Shaanxi, Qinghai, Xinjiang, Hebei, Henan, Hubei,
Hunan, and Jiangxi.

U.S. Consulate General, Chengdu

4 Lingshiguan Road
Section 4, Renmin Nanlu,
Chengdu, Sichuan 610041, China
Tel: (86-28) 8558-3992, 8558-9646
After hours/Emergencies: (86) 137-0800-1422
Fax: (86-28) 8556-5356
Email: ConsularChengdu@state.gov
This consular district includes the following provinces/regions
of China: Guizhou, Sichuan, Xizang (Tibet), and Yunnan, as well
as the municipality of Chongqing.

U.S. Consulate General, Guangzhou

1 South Shamian Street
Shamian Island 200S1
Guangzhou, Guangdong 510133, China
Tel: (020) 8121-8000
After hours/Emergencies: (020) 8121-6077
Fax: (020) 8121-9001
This consular district includes the following provinces/regions
of China: Guangdong, Guangxi, Hainan, and Fujian.

U.S. Consulate General, Shanghai
1469 Huai Hai Zhong Road
Shanghai 200031, China
Tel: (86-21) 6433-6880
Citizen Services: Westgate Mall
1038 West Nanjing Rd, 8th Fl.
Tel: (86-21) 3217-4650,
    extensions 2102, 2103, 2114
Fax: (86-21) 6217-2071
After-hours/Emergencies: (86-21) 6433-3936
Email: ShanghaiACS@state.gov
This consular district includes the following provinces/regions
of China: Shanghai, Anhui, Jiangsu, and Zhejiang.

U.S. Consulate General, Shenyang
52, 14th Wei Road
Heping District
Shenyang, Liaoning 110003, China
Tel: (86-24) 2322-1198
After-hours/Emergencies: (86-10) 6532-1910
Fax: (86-24) 2322-2374
This consular district includes the following
provinces/regions of China: Liaoning, Heilongjiang, and Jilin.

U.S. Consulate in Hong Kong
http://hongkong.usconsulate.gov

U.S. Consulate General, Hong Kong & Macao
26 Garden Road, Central
Hong Kong, China
Tel: (852) 2523-9011, Citizen Services (852) 2841-2211, 2323, 2225
After hours/Emergencies: (852) 2523-9011: follow prompts
Fax: (852) 2845-1598, Visa inquiries (852) 2845-4845
Email: information_resource_center_hk@yahoo.com
Email for visa issues: questions@hongkongacs.com
This consular district includes Hong Kong and Macao.

The Embassy of Canada to China
19 Dong Zhi Men Wai Street, Chaoyang District
Beijing 100600, China
Tel: (011-86-10) 6532-3536
Fax: (011-86-10) 6532-4072
E-mail: infocentrechina@international.gc.ca
Website: www.china.gc.ca

The Consulate General of Canada, Guangzhou
Suite 801, China Hotel Office Tower Liu Hua Lu
Guangzhou 510015, China
Tel: (011-86-20) 8666-0569
Fax: (011-86-20) 8668-6093
E-mail: guangzhou-commerce@international.gc.ca
Website: www.guangzhou.gc.ca

The Consulate General of Canada, Shanghai
Shanghai Centre, Suite 604, 1376 Nanjing Xi Lu
Shanghai 200040, China
Tel: (011-86-21) 6279-8400
Fax: (011-86-21) 6279-7456
E-mail: shngi-td@international.gc.ca
Website: www.infoexport.gc.ca/cn

The Consulate of Canada, Chongqing
Suite 1705, Metropolitan Tower
Wu Yi Road Yu Zhong District
Chongqing 400010, China
Tel: (011-86-23) 6373-8007
Fax: (86-23) 6373-8026
E-mail: chonq@international.gc.ca
Website: www.chongqing.gc.ca

Appendix B

Administrative Divisions and Major Cities

Anhui Province – Capital: Hefei
Major Cities: Huangshan, Bengbu, Maanshan, Tongling, Wuhu

Beijing: Capital of China

Chongqing (Municipality): (Newly Promoted as Municipality in 1997. It used to be a major city in Sichuan Province.)

Fujian Province – Capital: Fuzhou
Major Cities: Xiamen, Zhangzhou

Gansu Province – Capital: Lanzhou
Major Cities: Dunhuang, Jiayuguan

Guangdong Province – Capital: Guangzhou
Major Cities: Chaozhou, Dongguan, Shantou, Shenzhen, Shunde, Zhuhai

Guangxi Zhuang Autonomous Region – Capital: Nanning
Major Cities: Beihai, Guilin, Liuzhou

Guizhou Province – Capital: Guiyang
Major Cities: Anshun, Zunyi

Hainan Province – Capital: Haikou
Major Cities: Sanya

Hebei Province – Capital: Shijiazhuang
Major Cities: Cangzhou, Chengde, Qinhuangdao, Tangshan, Baoding, Zhangjiakou

Heilongjiang Province – Capital: Harbin
Major Cities: Hailaer, Mohe, Mudanjiang, Qiqihar, Suifenhe

Henan Province – Capital: Zhengzhou
Major Cities: Anyang, Kaifeng, Luoyang, Sanmenxia

Hong Kong Special Administrative Region (HKSAR)

Hubei Province – Capital: Wuhan
Major Cities: Huangshi, Shiyan, Shashi, Xiangfan, Yichang

79

Hunan Province – Capital: Changsha
Major Cities: Changde, Dayong, Hengyang, Xiangtan, Zhangjiajie

Inner Mongolia Autonomous Region – Capital: Hohhot
Major Cities: Baotou, Chifeng, Wuhai

Longmen Shiku (Dragon Gate Grottoes), or the Longmen Grottoes, are a series of caves carved out of a mountainside in Luoyang, Henan Province; it is a UNESCO World Cultural Heritage Site. There are more than 2,000 grottoes with more than 100,000 statues and 3,600 inscriptions. Considered to be the zenith of Chinese stone carving, it is the largest collection of Chinese Buddhist art of the Northern Wei and Tang Dynasties (316-907).

Jiangsu Province – Capital: Nanjing
Major Cities: Lianyungang, Xuzhou, Suzhou, Wuxi, Zhenjiang

Jiangxi Province – Capital: Nanchang
Major Cities: Jiujiang, Lushan, Jian, Jinggangshan

Jilin Province – Capital: Changchun
Major Cities: Jilin, Tuman, Yanji

Liaoning Province – Capital: Shenyang
Major Cities: Dalian, Dandong, Anshan, Wafangdian

Ningxia Hui Autonomous Region – Capital: Yinchuan
Major City: Shizuishan

Qinghai Province – Capital: Xining

Shaanxi Province – Capital: Xi'an
(It used to be China's ancient capital, called Chang An.)
Major Cities: Xianyang, Baoji, Hanzhong

Shandong Province – Capital: Jinan
Major Cities: Dezhou, Linyi, Qingdao, Qufu, Tai'an, Yantai

Shanghai (Municipality): (The largest city in China.)

Shanxi Province – Capital: Taiyuan
Major Cities: Datong, Linfen, Yangquan

Sichuan Province – Capital: Chengdu
Major Cities: Emeishan, Zigong, Daxianshi

Taiwan Province – Major Cities: Taipei, Gaoxiong, Tainan, Xinzhu

Tianjin (Municipality)

Tibet Autonomous Region – Capital: Lhasa
Major City: Xigaze

Xinjiang Uygur Autonomous Region – Capital: Urumqi
Area: 1,600,000 square kilometers
Population: 16.89 million
Major Cities: Kashgar, Turfan

Yunnan Province – Capital: Kunming
Area: 394,000 square kilometers
Population: 40.42 million
Major Cities: Dali, Simao, Xishuangbanna

Macao Special Administrative Region (MSAR)

Zhejiang Province – Capital: Hangzhou
Major Cities: Jiaxing, Ningbo, Shaoxing, Wenzhou

Note: **Hong Kong and Macao:**

Hong Kong and Macao were part of China during ancient times and were taken by Britain and Portugal respectively following the Opium War of 1840. Hong Kong returned to Chinese sovereignty on July 1, 1997, and China resumed its exercise of sovereignty over Macao on December 20, 1999. The official names of both are: Hong Kong Special Administrative Region (HKSAR) and the Macao Special Administrative Region (MSAR).

Appendix C

Chronology of Chinese History

Period of the Five Legendary Rulers: 2600 B.C.E. – 2070 B.C.E.: Huang-di (or Yellow Emperor), Zhuanxu, Kiku, Yao, Shun			
Xia Dynasty			2070-1600 B.C.E.
Shang Dynasty			1600-1046 B.C.E.
Zhou Dynasty	**Western**		1046-771 B.C.E.
	Eastern		770-256 B.C.E.
	Spring and Autumn Period		770-476 B.C.E.
	Warring States Period		475-221 B.C.E.
Qin Dynasty			221-206 B.C.E.
Han Dynasty	**Western Han**		206 B.C.E-C.E 25
	Eastern Han		25-220
Three Kingdoms	**Wei**		220-265
	Shu Han		221-263
	Wu		222-280
Western Jin Dynasty			265-317
Eastern Jin Dynasty			317-420
Northern and Southern Dynasty	**Southern Dynasty**	**Song**	420-479
		Qi	479-502
		Liang	502-557
	Northern Dynasty	**Northern Wei**	386-534
		Eastern Wei	534-550
		Northern Qi	550-577
		Western Wei	535-556
		Northern Zhou	557-581
Sui Dynasty			581-618

Chronology of Chinese History

Tang Dynasty		581-618
Five Dynasty	Later Liang	907-923
	Later Tang	923-936
	Later Jin	936-947
	Later Han	947-950
	Later Zhou	951-960
Song Dynasty	Northern Song	960-1127
	Southern Song	1127-1279
Liao Dynasty		907-1125
Jin Dynasty		1115-1234
Yuan Dynasty		1206-1368
Ming Dynasty		1368-1644
Qing Dynasty		1616-1911
Republic of China		1912-1949
People's Republic of China		1949-

Two of the Founders of Ancient China

*Huang-di, **the Yellow Emperor,** was the first of the first five legendary rulers of China (2600 B.C.E. to 2070 B.C.E.). He is called the common ancestor of the Chinese people. His name was Gongsun. Starting with a kingdom by the Yellow River, through a series of battles, he became "lord of the world." According to myth, after bringing peace to the world, he invented the calendar, mathematics, music, medicine, metallurgy, and Chinese writing. At 100, he left the throne to become immortal.*

*Zheng became the king of the Qin clan in 247 B.C.E., at the age of twelve. In 238 at 21, he seized control, and by 221 he had defeated all of the Warring States and declared himself Qin Shi Huangdi, **The First Emperor of Qin,** taking the title Huangdi used by the Yellow Emperor. He had united all of China, all of the known, civilized world. He immediately started to build his tomb, filled with a huge terra cotta army, and to connect walls of earlier kingdoms into the Great Wall of China. He built an imperial capital city, Xianyang, and standardized the written language, the currency, and the use of weights and measures. Surppressing the influence of Confucius, he ruled with strict, brutal laws and by keeping a large living army to control and expand his empire. He died in 210.*

Two views of the Forbidden City, Beijing

The Forbidden City was the Imperial Palace ruling China from 1420 in the Ming Dynasty until the end of the Empire and the beginning of the Republic in 1912. Then the last Emperor, Puyi of the Qing Dynasty, lived there until 1924, when he was banished. The huge compound with 980 buildings is surrounded by a wall and moat. Nobody was allowed within these walls without the Emperor's permission, which is why it was called "Forbidden." It has been looted several times, and during the Cultural Revolution it might have been destroyed, like much of China's cultural heritage, if Primier Zhou Enlai hadn't sent an army battalion to protect it.